# Dilemma-based Learning in the Humanities

## Integrating social, emotional and thinking skills

**Phil Wood, Barry Hymer & Deborah Michel**

© Phil Wood, Barry Hymer & Deborah Michel
2007

ISBN 978-1-899857-54-8

Published 2007 by Chris Kington Publishing an imprint of Optimus Education,
a division of Optimus Professional Publishing Limited. Registered office:
33-41 Dallington Street, London EC1V 0BB. Registered in England and Wales.
Registration number: 05791519

www.teachingexpertise.com

British Library cataloguing in publication data. A catalogue record for this book is
available from the British Library.

Printed and bound by:
The Charlesworth Group, Wakefield, UK
www.charlesworth.com

Edited by:
Giles Flitney

Designed by:
Character Design, Hereford, England.

Cover illustration and design by:
Geoff Read

# Foreword

Life and learning are only neat in the minds of planners. For the rest of us, especially teachers, they are full of ambiguities and in such a context it is no surprise that dilemmas arise. But the dominant pattern of classroom life does not easily embrace dilemmas, even though there are many good reasons for doing so.

In classrooms, we know that open-ended sometimes ambiguous tasks generate increased engagement, yet we also find that in current times teachers are encouraged or pressured to over-engineer classrooms, with negative consequences for students' sense of responsibility towards their own learning.

We also know that classroom tasks which are open-ended and ill-structured not only require higher-level thinking, they also promote collaboration because mutual interchange is a necessary condition for solving the problem.

So the aspects of classroom and learning life which unfortunately are so often separated – the social, emotional and thinking aspects – are promoted together within the approach, being seen as part of the same overall approach to learning within the classroom.

Help in running a classroom in an engaging and authentic fashion is always welcome. This book is particularly welcome since it supports teachers with one of their own central dilemmas: how to release control of certain processes in the classroom and yet be confident that learning is developing from it. This is one of the challenges of creating learning environments that encourage student responsibility.

The frameworks for exploring dilemmas and for reviewing the process provided here are very valuable, especially since it is in the process of review where the richest learning occurs. Moreover, the frameworks are not straitjackets, and the support which this book offers on taking dilemma-based learning further is well-judged.

Unlike many of the prescriptions which are offered to teachers nowadays, the practices in this book are well founded in up-to-date conceptualisation and evidence, and promise to make a significant contribution to effective learning in classrooms. Humanities teachers who operate classrooms in the fashion which is supported here, will not only find a richer version of classroom life, but may also reclaim some important professional satisfaction.

Chris Watkins

Reader in Education, University of London Institute of Education

*Classrooms as Learning Communities: what's in it for schools,* Routledge 2005

*Effective Learning in Classrooms,* with Carnell E and Lodge C, Sage 2007

# Contents

Chris Kington Publishing

# The authors

Dr Phil Wood spent a number of years teaching in the wilds of the Lincolnshire Wolds before moving to Market Deeping, Lincolnshire where he led a geography department for five years, also qualifying as an AST, and working with colleagues in local schools. In autumn 2005, he started to work part-time at the School of Education, University of Leicester, going full time in Autumn 2006, acting as the geography PGCE tutor, as well as teaching on a number of other courses, with special interests in learning and assessment.

Dr Barry Hymer is a former secondary and primary school teacher and LA educational psychologist, who currently practises as a freelance teacher, speaker and writer. He is the director of Still Thinking UK Ltd and a visiting fellow at Newcastle University's Centre for Teaching and Learning. www.barryhymer.co.uk

Deborah Michel is a senior adviser within the National Strategy leading on Social and Emotional Aspects of Learning (SEAL) in both primary and secondary school. She has been a key contributor to the development and writing of both Primary and Secondary SEAL. Deborah is by profession an educational psychologist with a long interest in social and emotional skills. In 1994 she devised the Cumbria Behaviour Curriculum, a whole-school approach to promoting social and emotional skills, and worked with colleagues in schools to develop materials to support it. She has long experience within education having taught in primary, secondary and special schools then as an educational psychologist. She was co-author of a successful series of text books, Headwork, published by Oxford University Press in 1984.

Chris Kington Publishing

# Introduction

*Ah well, homework then. He turned the screen off and reached reluctantly for his schoolbag. Half of it was geography, which was nearly all colouring in and copying and drawing. Kid's work. He had thought that the colouring would stop when he was at secondary school, but no such luck. Resignedly he pulled the folder towards him and started to shade in a patch of steppe... He put the finishing touches to 'Africa – Main Crops' and looked with disfavour at 'Africa – Climate.' One day, work and life would not be this boring.*

(Libby Purves, *Passing Go*, 2000)

Many of the issues that are considered in the humanities are complex in nature. They require us to consider them from a number of different perspectives, and on a regular basis we ask students to grapple with issues that have no clearly defined solutions – in other words, they are asked to consider, and perhaps even suggest, solutions to dilemmas. The definition of a dilemma is that there is no single 'correct' and definable solution and, as such, we cannot give students ready packaged systems to follow to help them make the correct decision each time. However, by aiding them to understand the multifaceted and complex nature of dilemmas we can help them develop their ability to make wise choices that they can both understand and explain.

The ideas and materials in this book arose out of a series of group enquiries held in Barrow-in-Furness, in south-west Cumbria. Section 4 of this book details the theoretical and practical origins of the approach, but for our present purposes we have decided to avoid any lengthy preamble, and invite you to delve straight in to working with dilemmas in your secondary humanities classroom. In keeping with the spirit of the approach, however, we invite you to develop a praxis that involves both reflection and action in equal measure, and in harmony.

## How this book is arranged

The book is split into four sections, which have been written to develop an understanding of the ways in which the dilemma-based learning framework can be applied to secondary humanities classrooms. Each section has several foci that encourage a critical understanding of the techniques and how they can be developed and used in the classroom. Each of the first three sections includes:

- a simple continuing professional development element, which has been designed for use by individuals, small groups, or whole staff meetings – this highlights some of the main ideas and approaches found within that section
- a consideration of how dilemma-based learning sessions can be facilitated within the classroom
- a number of suggested dilemmas covering geography, history and religious education
- suggestions for developing your own dilemmas
- a consideration of how the approach can positively affect students
- how dilemma-based learning can be applied beyond and between classrooms
- a simple framework for reviewing and planning for further development of the technique.

The four sections are also focused as follows:

- **Section 1:** Focusing on the basic nature of dilemma-based learning. An introduction to basic dilemmas and the frameworks that can be developed to enable their successful use.

- **Section 2:** Developing the use of dilemmas as a basis for learning, together with a more complex set of ideas to bring depth to learning and aid the development of wise choices.

- **Section 3:** Enhancing the use of dilemmas through the use of ethical and sophisticated thinking techniques with students, and the use of the ideas developed to aid students outside the classroom and school.

- Finally, **Section 4** considers some of the learning theory that provides the psychological and philosophical basis for the dilemma-based learning technique.

This outline is shown in diagrammatic form on the next page, and the individual elements are repeated at the start of each section.

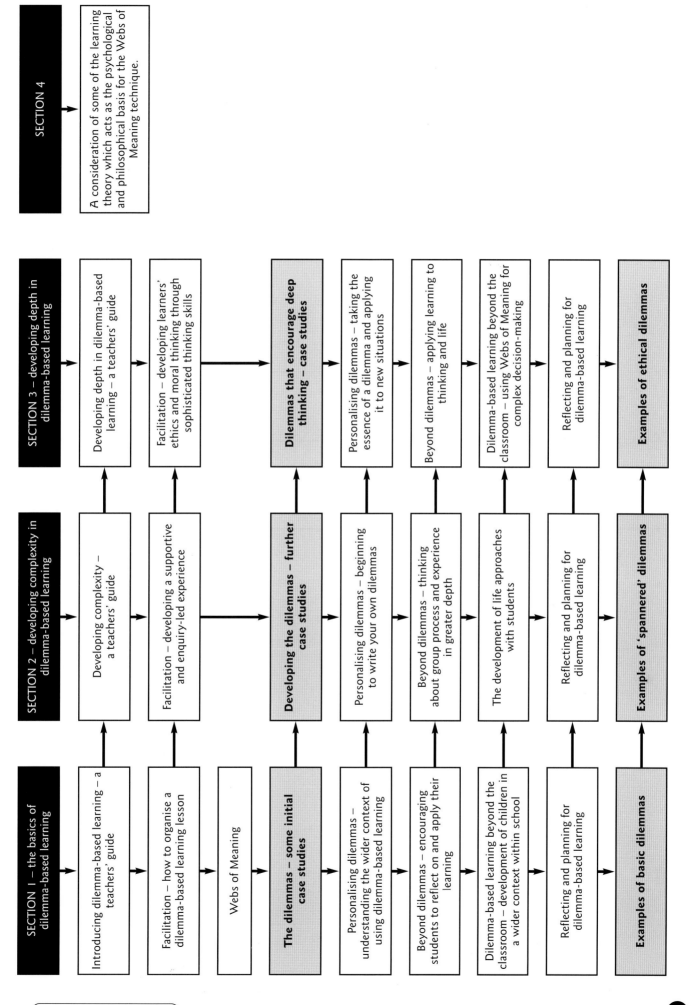

**SECTION 4**

A consideration of some of the learning theory which acts as the psychological and philosophical basis for the Webs of Meaning technique.

**SECTION 3 – developing depth in dilemma-based learning**

Developing depth in dilemma-based learning – a teachers' guide

Facilitation – developing learners' ethics and moral thinking through sophisticated thinking skills

**Dilemmas that encourage deep thinking – case studies**

Personalising dilemmas – taking the essence of a dilemma and applying it to new situations

Beyond dilemmas – applying learning to thinking and life

Dilemma-based learning beyond the classroom – using Webs of Meaning for complex decision-making

Reflecting and planning for dilemma-based learning

**Examples of ethical dilemmas**

**SECTION 2 – developing complexity in dilemma-based learning**

Developing complexity – a teachers' guide

Facilitation – developing a supportive and enquiry-led experience

**Developing the dilemmas – further case studies**

Personalising dilemmas – beginning to write your own dilemmas

Beyond dilemmas – thinking about group process and experience in greater depth

The development of life approaches with students

Reflecting and planning for dilemma-based learning

**Examples of 'spannered' dilemmas**

**SECTION 1 – the basics of dilemma-based learning**

Introducing dilemma-based learning – a teachers' guide

Facilitation – how to organise a dilemma-based learning lesson

Webs of Meaning

**The dilemmas – some initial case studies**

Personalising dilemmas – understanding the wider context of using dilemma-based learning

Beyond dilemmas – encouraging students to reflect on and apply their learning

Dilemma-based learning beyond the classroom – development of children in a wider context within school

Reflecting and planning for dilemma-based learning

**Examples of basic dilemmas**

# The basics of dilemma-based learning

# The basics of dilemma-based learning

Section 1 focuses on introducing the basic format and approach of dilemma-based learning. This is intended for those who are coming to the approach for the first time and those who want to understand the basics.

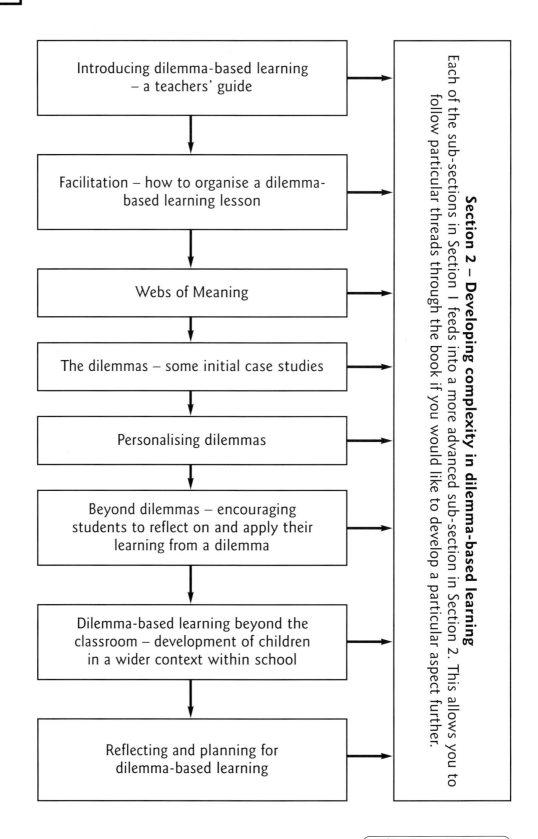

Introducing dilemma-based learning – a teachers' guide

Facilitation – how to organise a dilemma-based learning lesson

Webs of Meaning

The dilemmas – some initial case studies

Personalising dilemmas

Beyond dilemmas – encouraging students to reflect on and apply their learning from a dilemma

Dilemma-based learning beyond the classroom – development of children in a wider context within school

Reflecting and planning for dilemma-based learning

**Section 2 – Developing complexity in dilemma-based learning**
Each of the sub-sections in Section 1 feeds into a more advanced sub-section in Section 2. This allows you to follow particular threads through the book if you would like to develop a particular aspect further.

# Introducing dilemma-based learning – a teachers' guide

> **Aims**
>
> - To introduce the Web of Meaning
> - To introduce the basic structure of Webs of Meaning
> - To highlight possible ways to begin to integrate Webs of Meaning into the curriculum and beyond

> **Timings for training session**
>
> - Introducing dilemmas and the thinking skills associated with them (*20 minutes*)
> - Introducing the dilemma-based learning structure and its relation to thinking skills (*20 minutes*)
> - Considering how dilemma-based learning can begin to be used in a school environment (*20 minutes*)

## Dilemma-based learning – an introduction to the concept of dilemmas

Dilemma-based learning is an approach to thinking that focuses on the use of dilemmas to develop an individual's thinking skills. Consider the passage below:

> *You know you are an excellent subject teacher. Your classes are well organised, and you genuinely enjoy the excitement of working with young people and trying out new ideas in the classroom. Your partner hates his/her job and would love to undertake a period of full-time study leading to a change of career. If this were to happen, your family finances would be very tight.*
>
> *A job is advertised at your school, and you know that you have a very good chance of getting it. However, it will take you out of the classroom, and burden you with greater management and administrative responsibilities. You'd enjoy these stresses much less than teaching – but the money would be good...*

**Q** Having read through this dilemma consider what your solution might be, either individually or through group discussion. Once you have done this, consider the types of thinking and associated skills you are asked to utilise.

## Possible answers

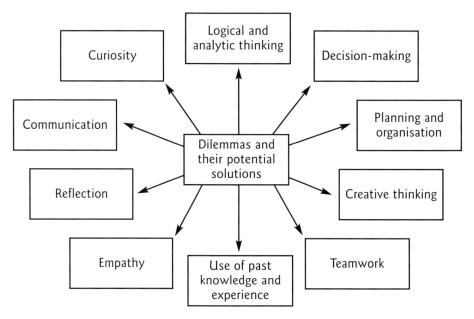

As this collection of thinking skills exemplifies, dilemma-based learning is a technique that has been developed to aid affective and high order thinking, particularly in a group situation. It does this by using dilemmas as a vehicle for allowing students the time and space to think and come up with a series of different, potentially conflicting, solutions to issues. One of the most important factors in developing this critical and creative climate is the realisation that a dilemma can be classed as such due to the lack of a clear-cut solution to the issue.

## Introducing the Web of Meaning

As with any thinking skills exercise, the aim is to aid and guide students to develop a skill. As such, a framework makes the thinking more focused, especially in the early period of developing a set of skills. To aid discussion and thinking with regards to dilemmas, the Web of Meaning, together with its subsets, offers such a framework.

**Q** **Using the diagram opposite, think/discuss what you believe the foci of the four smaller Webs of Meaning might be. If you assume that a number of questions are connected to each of the four, try to develop a list or mind map that details questions that might fit each area. You might want to use the dilemma you have already considered as a guide.**

> Now have a look at p8-13 to see what has already been suggested.
> You might want to add some of your own if you feel they are suitable.

## Using dilemma-based learning in the classroom

Having considered the essential features behind the dilemma-based learning approach, you can now take the idea further and discuss how such an approach might be used in classrooms. You might want to refer back to the outline of Section 1 on p2. Then consider the questions on p24 in the section headed 'Personalising dilemmas'. Try the approach at some time in the near future, then have a discussion or think about some of the questions and thoughts posed in the section 'Reflecting and planning for dilemma-based learning' on p35.

# The Web of Meaning

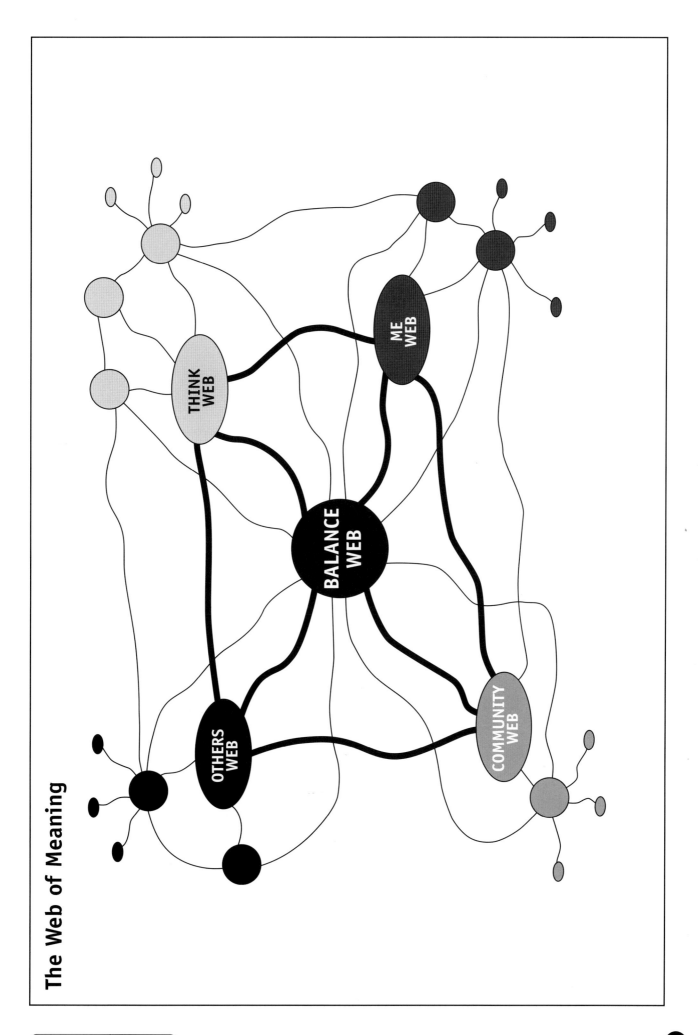

# Facilitation – how to organise a dilemma-based learning lesson

## Using the dilemmas

GO TO ⋯➤

For further detail on other potential uses of the technique go to p14.

Although the dilemmas in this book are specifically created for location in a particular area of the secondary humanities curriculum, they are intended, as a general principle, **to encourage group enquiry into what it means to make a wise choice as a young person** – in the context of home and school. The chief value of the process lies not in the acquisition of content knowledge (although this will invariably happen), but in the learning-to-learn skills and dispositions acquired and developed en route to the resolution of the dilemma. There is no one way to use the dilemmas and, whilst the focus of the present book is on the dilemma-based learning process (which is outlined below), they are also ideal for use as a stimulus in many other contexts.

## Ways of running a dilemma-based learning lesson

*Think wrongly if you please, but in all cases think for yourself*
                    Doris Lessing

Dilemma-based learning is an approach that can be used in a range of environments, including whole-class situations and enrichment or extension withdrawal groups. The most likely way to use the dilemmas and Webs is with a whole class. The standard approach is discussed in more detail below, but in brief:

- students work in enquiry groups of four to seven members per group
- all groups address the same dilemma
- each group's task is collaboratively to seek the wisest possible solution to a dilemma
- it is stressed that there may be no one 'right' response to the dilemma, and that the teacher does not hold any such 'right' response in his/her head
- it is possible that each group will come up with a different solution
- what is being asked for is careful consideration of the core issues involved, and decisions that are informed by reflection and reason.

The groups might be asked to use one or more of the Webs of Meaning to facilitate their thinking. When the groups have discovered their wisest possible solution, they can usefully come together as a whole-class group to question each other about the wisdom of their solution and about how well they have enquired together.

## A suggested plan for a whole-class dilemma-based learning session

### Preliminaries

GO TO ⋯➤

For further consideration of the factors relating to the development of Webs of Meaning go to p16.

The ease with which students take to dilemma-based learning will depend, to a large extent, on their prior experiences of collaborative learning and groupwork. Classes with little such experience will require higher levels of adult facilitation, and in such cases dilemma-based learning is best introduced over time, in adult-facilitated groups. In addition to the class teacher, facilitation might also be available from teaching assistants, parents, older adults (eg Age Concern volunteers) and older students. Whilst dilemma-based learning is an effective tool for teaching group skills, it shouldn't be attempted without skilled adult facilitation when the students lack the pre-skills necessary for effective groupwork – basic levels of trust, respect, turn-taking skills, etc are required, and in extreme cases these might need introducing through an appropriate programme of intervention prior to the introduction of dilemma-based learning.

It is important that the class is explicitly aware of the main purpose of dilemma-based learning: that is – to help them to practise and to develop their abilities to make wise choices in their lives. This is done by experiencing enquiries into a number of difficult choices based upon real life. Enquiries are based upon a joint quest – in the belief that several thinkers working together are more effective than just one. A secondary purpose is for the students to improve their group skills. During dilemma-based learning lessons they will have an opportunity to reflect upon their progress in both these areas of development.

## Suggested stages

**Whole-class calming activity:** This is to ensure that students are relaxed and focused. Such activities might include a few minutes of guided visualisation, a stilling activity with background music on, or uninterrupted silent reading.

**Whole-class introduction of the dilemma:** The whole class starts together. The dilemma is introduced, either by the teacher or by a volunteer. Key points in relation to the dilemma are suggested by the students and written on the white-board, possibly in the form of a mind map.

**Small-group activity:** The class then divides up into small groups (four to seven students in each) to enquire into and decide together upon the wisest possible solution to the dilemma, using the Webs of Meaning to structure their thinking. To start with, it may be necessary for roles to be allocated, but over time the groups can become increasingly autonomous. Whilst there is no specific requirement to apportion particular roles within each group, group members might, for instance, be given one or more of these specific roles:

GO TO ⋯⟫

The Webs of Meaning are further explained on p8.

- **A Web master** – to keep the group on track and to remind students to speak within the terms of the Web that is currently on the table. The Web master manages the Webs, keeps the discussion moving in liaison with a facilitator (see below) and ensures that the group move on to the next Web at an appropriate point.

- **A timekeeper** – to keep an eye on the time and to ensure that choices are made within the time available.

- **A group facilitator** – to keep track of how the group is working together and to ensure that the group is seeking the best possible solution rather than becoming distracted by personal issues. Mediation skills might be needed to play this role effectively.

- **An observer** – to notice the group interactions, and to feed back on group processes during the review session (see Beyond dilemmas, p28).

- **A scout** – to eavesdrop discreetly on other groups' discussions and to report back on useful ideas and pertinent considerations (a popular role for students with high energy levels/kinaesthetic learning styles!) This role should be outlined carefully – and groups should not see students playing this role as 'cheats': groups are not working competitively against each other, but collaboratively with each other.

The Webs are, in turn, placed in the middle of the group and used as a focus for the discussion and resolution of the dilemma.

**Individual and group reflection activity:** When the group has decided upon the wisest solution, individual members might fill in the process review sheet, which has been designed to help students to evaluate the quality of the enquiry and of the group processes. Having completed the review sheet individually, members might get back together to discuss how well they enquired as a group.

GO TO ⋯⟫

Find a copy of a process review sheet on p29.

**Content plenary:** To finish this stage of the lesson, the whole class might get back together to share their solutions. Groups might be provided with an opportunity to question other groups about their ideas. When all the groups have shared their ideas, the class might like to vote on their agreed solution to the dilemma. The lessons should end with a discussion about the quality of the groups' enquiries and the identification of learning points for next time.

GO TO ⋯⟫

The section on process review can be found on p28.

# The Webs of Meaning

The Webs of Meaning are a scaffolding technique that has been developed to aid students' thinking and discussion. **[NB Each group in the class should have access to a set, available as a photocopiable resource on p167-173 and on the CD-Rom that accompanies this book.]**

There are five core Webs, plus a Reflection Web. The Webs of Meaning provide a visual reminder to help structure students' thinking about a dilemma, as they are associated with questions to facilitate and support group enquiry. The Webs are best used in groups of four to seven students, but with an adult facilitator they can be used in larger groups. There can be value in the teacher playing a more directive role in talking through a 'practice' dilemma with the students – modelling the process with the whole-class group, but inviting the students to suggest possibilities, reasons, flaws, etc.

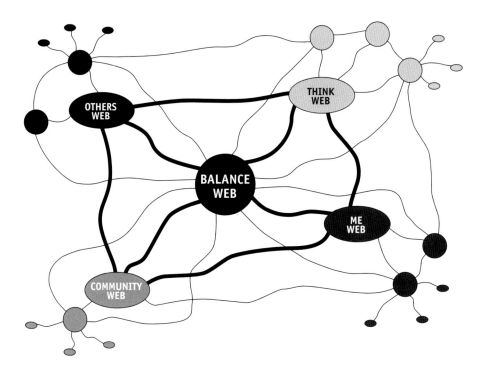

*Chris Kington Publishing*

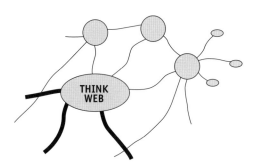

# The Think Web

This Web has three main elements that encourage thinking and reflection. The first step should be an opportunity for reflection and analysis of the key issues and elements of the dilemma under enquiry. Key issues might be listed on a whiteboard. Key questions to prompt these issues include:

- Is this a dilemma? What makes this a dilemma?
- What are the key issues that might influence a solution?
- How does this dilemma resemble something I've encountered before?

The second step is to generate as many solutions to the dilemma as possible. The primary aim here is to be as creative as possible. Key questions to spark this discussion could include:

- How many solutions can we find?
- Can any solutions be linked or connected in some way, to form yet another solution?
- Can we think of any more unusual ideas?

The third step is to select the three most practical solutions through logical and analytical thought. Key questions include:

- Are any of the solutions clearly unrealistic? Are you sure? How do you know this?
- What exactly is involved in each solution?
- What would happen if this were to be done?
- How would we know if it were successful?
- What would happen if we tried and failed?
- How likely is it to be successful?
- Which three shall we choose?
- What are the costs – time, money, etc?

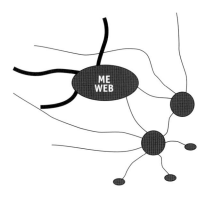

# The Me Web

The first step is to establish each group member's personal feelings. It might be that some members are feeling hard done by because their ideas were not listened to, or they might have some personal experience that is relevant to the dilemma but has not yet emerged. Key questions to ask include:

- How does everyone feel about the choice of solutions?
- Are there any objections to the choices made by the group? On what grounds?
- Do you have anything you wish to say from your own point of view or experience?

The second step is to explore each of the chosen options from the perspective of the central character in the dilemma.

- How would he or she feel?
- What would it mean for him or her?
- What would happen to him or her as a result of the actions?

One member of the group might take the role of the central character of the dilemma for the discussion.

*NB: The Me Web and Others Web might be used together. Sometimes certain Webs get covered naturally by students before they are explicitly introduced, eg students often range onto Community Web issues whilst addressing the Others Web. This is natural and in many senses desirable as students become more familiar and confident with the approach; teachers should exercise their own judgements as to whether or not a strict sequence of administration of the Webs is appropriate – flexibility will often be required.*

# The Others Web

The first step is to identify which other characters might be affected by the dilemma or the solutions identified. Key questions include:

- Who else is mentioned in the dilemma?
- Is there anyone else who might be affected, but who isn't specifically mentioned?

The second step is to explore the dilemma from the perspective of each of the minor characters identified, examining each of the three 'solutions' in turn. Key questions include:

- What would happen to the character?
- How would the character feel?
- How would the character feel if he or she found out what had happened?
- What would each character like to happen?
- What does each character know about the dilemma and the suggested solution?

This might be done as a group, or each group member might discuss these questions when taking on the role of one of the characters in the story.

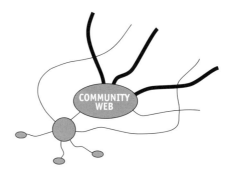

# The Community Web

This Web provides an opportunity for the group to explore what the various options might mean for the community as a whole. A community in this sense might be a class, a school, a family, a housing estate, a town/city, the country or world. Key questions include:

- What would happen if everyone chose to do this?
- What would people think about the family/class/school?
- How would the situation look to other people?
- What would happen in the long term to the family/class/school?
- What might other people in the community learn from what had happened?

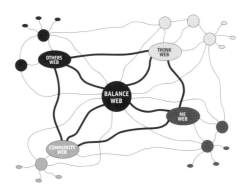

# The Balance Web

This Web is always the last Web to be tabled. It aims to allow time for a reflective and balanced choice. An intuitive response might be most appropriate. Intuition is often at its sharpest after periods of reflection and contemplation.

The first step is for the group members to reflect individually on their intuitive choices.

The second step is for each member of the group to specify his or her preferred option. The other group members should listen carefully and say nothing whilst other members are speaking.

If there is no consensus, each person should have an opportunity to restate his or her preferred option – providing reasons. Other members of the group might pose questions to explore the implications of the solution from a range of perspectives. Key questions include:

- What would happen if this solution worked?
- What might go wrong and why?
- What might happen if the solution went wrong?
- How likely is it that the solution might go wrong?
- How likely is it that the solution would work?
- Is the solution practical?

If there is a consensus, a quick review of the implications of the chosen solution might take place by working through the previous Webs.

## Other potential uses of the technique

### As a stimulus for a community of enquiry – eg Philosophy for Children (P4C)

You might read the dilemma to the class group and encourage the students to discuss and agree in pairs the 'best' possible solution to the dilemma. After sharing their ideas in a brief whole-class plenary, the students would be asked to generate their own questions – questions that they would like to use for a class-based enquiry. [For readers unfamiliar with the process of P4C (Philosophy for Children), the SAPERE website is recommended as a starting point for acquiring further skills and information – see **www.sapere.org.uk**]

### As a stimulus for a citizenship or PSHE lesson

Dilemmas lend themselves to these areas of the secondary curriculum, as they invite students to invest their own experiences, views and beliefs into the context of pair-work, small group and whole-class discussions.

### As a stimulus for circle time

Whilst this approach is more frequently encountered in primary schools, it is increasingly acknowledged as having a role to play in the secondary school environment too. The facilitator reads or asks the class to read the dilemma. The participants in the circle suggest possible solutions to the dilemma. Alternatively, the participants might work in small groups to discuss possible solutions that they share in the circle.

### As a stimulus for a drama lesson

In groups, the class might be asked to role-play the characters in the dilemma and generate as many possible solutions and their outcomes as they can. This approach lends itself to the 'hot-seating' of key characters.

# The dilemmas – some initial case studies

GO TO ⋯⟫

For a consideration of how to develop your own dilemmas see Section 2, p77.

In this section a number of basic dilemmas are presented to introduce the use of the classroom-based technique outlined in the previous section. Each dilemma is presented as a case study of how the technique might fit into classroom pedagogy.

---

**History**                                                          **Case Study 1**

*This dilemma is intended to take much of the cultural baggage away from the rise of Hitler, so that students are forced to consider their own perspective on the position of politicians in Germany between the World Wars. Again, it might best act as an introduction to studying the rise of Hitler.*

---

You are the leader of a minor political party in a central European country and are on the verge of attaining some real power. Your advisors tell you that you have one clear opportunity to take power.

You believe that taking control would allow you to play a crucial role in developing your society and economy, as it has been ravaged by war and industrial collapse. Not only that, but neighbouring governments are constantly watching over your country.

However, to enable you to take the reins of power your advisors tell you that you will need to break the law and manipulate parliament.

Your move.

## Introducing the dilemma

Having settled the group with some form of simple starter activity, introduce the information given on p15 on the whiteboard, and on copied sheets for the students. The dilemma should be read through and the students asked to spend a few minutes quietly considering the main pieces of information they have been given. Once this has been reflected upon, the students should then be invited to build a simple list or mind map on the board that highlights the key points. In this case, the main issues focus on the ethics of power and the determination of national policy.

## Developing wisdom in groups

GO TO

The roles are given on p7.

Having explicitly introduced some of the factors that might play a major part in the students' deliberation, split them up into small groups to discuss the issues and to attempt to develop a wise solution. If the exercise is being taught for the first time, or where there is little experience of the technique, the teacher might want to ask students to allocate themselves various roles to facilitate the work of the group. However, if students have used this technique before, it might be better to allow them to organise themselves. Each group is given an opportunity to use each of the Webs in turn to help scaffold their discussion. In this case study, some of the pertinent questions to highlight for students might include:

### The Think Web

- What makes this a dilemma?
- What are the key issues that might influence a solution?
- How many solutions can we find?

### The Me Web

- How does everyone feel about the choice of solutions?
- What would it mean for him or her?

### The Others Web

- Is there anyone else who might be affected, but who isn't specifically mentioned?
- What would happen to that character?

### The Community Web

- What would happen in the various groups involved?
- How would this situation look to other people?

This process should be used to allow the group to agree on a solution that they believe to be the wisest.

## Reflection on the process

GO TO

Find a copy of a process review sheet on p29.

The group, having made their choice, should then be given an opportunity to reflect on the process they have been through. What is important here is that students have the chance to think through their own experience, and that of the group, properly. It is tempting to move through this element of the exercise quickly, but it is through this meta-cognitive discussion that the process of making wise choices has a real chance to develop. Therefore, students should fill in the process review sheet individually, and then come back together to discuss their work as a group. It might be useful on the first few occasions that the technique is used to list some particular areas for the students to consider on the whiteboard so that they have a clear structure to follow.

## The plenary

This stage of the exercise is an opportunity for students to share their experiences. Again, it should be as student-led as possible. Each group should be given the opportunity to present both their solution, and the reasoning behind their solution. It should also be possible for the other groups to question them about their work. Possible solutions might be written up on the board, and the main ideas behind them added. The students could then be asked to vote for the solution that they think is the wisest, and could be asked to discuss this in a follow-up piece of written work.

It is crucial, however, that as well as discussing the content, the process through which the solution was arrived at is also carefully and fully considered. This meta-level discussion will make explicit the thought and group processes involved and, through the use of a reflective diary or log, the ideas can be revisited the next time the technique is used, to help develop skills further and more directly.

It might then be useful to highlight that this might have been the choice facing Hitler in the 1930s. Then gain reactions from the students in terms of the difference that this makes to them, and also make clear that any situation can be made to sound 'value neutral'. They might therefore want to consider what the consequences of 'bending the rules' might be for other groups, and that the results of such decisions might only become apparent when it is too late.

## Timings

It is vital that the students have a clear opportunity to discuss and consider both the content and the process involved in making a wise decision. For this reason students should not be made to reach conclusions quickly. An exercise such as this should be taught over a full two lessons (of approximately one hour each).

## Religious education

*This dilemma takes the idea of planetary stewardship and puts it in a more localised context for the students. Should they look after the earth (which may curtail some of their enjoyment) or should they not worry, and enjoy life to the max?*

You have been left at home for the weekend by your parents whilst they visit relatives. Your parents have just had a week off work to spend time on their garden. They have laid a new lawn, and have planted a large number of new plants.

Unfortunately, they have chosen a week when the weather has been very dry and hot. They tell you that they need you to water the lawn and plants at least twice a day so that they don't die from the heat and lack of water.

They have your mobile number in case of emergency. Soon after they have left, a friend asks you if you will go to their house for the weekend as they are having a party on the Saturday evening. They are really keen for you to stay the night.

Decisions, decisions.

## Introducing the dilemma

Having settled the group with some form of starter exercise, such as an 'odd-one-out' exercise or other 'thought-showering' introduction, introduce the information given on p18 on the whiteboard, and on copied sheets for the students. The dilemma should be read through and the students asked to spend a few minutes quietly considering the main pieces of information they have been given. Once this has been reflected upon, the students should then be invited to build a simple list or mind map on the board that highlights the key points. In this case, this might include issues of rights and responsibilities, what it means to be part of a community, and our potential impact on our environment.

## Developing wisdom in groups

Having explicitly introduced some of the factors that might play a major part in the students' deliberation, split them up into small groups to discuss the issues and to attempt to develop a wise solution. If the exercise is being taught for the first time, or where there is little experience of the technique, the teacher might want to ask students to allocate themselves various roles to facilitate the work of the group. However, if students have used this technique before, it might be better to allow them to organise themselves. Each group is given an opportunity to use each of the Webs in turn to help scaffold their discussion. In this case study, some of the pertinent questions to highlight for students might include:

GO TO ⋯⟩

The roles are given on p7.

### The Think Web
- What makes this a dilemma?
- What are the key issues that might influence a solution?
- What exactly is involved in each solution?

### The Me Web
- How does everyone feel about the choice of solutions?
- What would happen to him or her as a result of the actions?

### The Others Web
- How would each character feel?
- What would each character like to happen?

### The Community Web
- What would happen if everyone chose to do this?
- What might other people in the community learn from what had happened?

This process should be used to allow the group to agree on a solution that they believe to be the wisest.

## Reflection on the process

The group, having made their choice, should then be given an opportunity to reflect on the process they have been through. What is important here is that students have the chance to think through their own experience, and that of the group, properly. It is tempting to move through this element of the exercise quickly, but it is through this meta-cognitive discussion that the process of making wise choices has a real chance to develop. Therefore, students should fill in the process review sheet individually, and then come back together to discuss their work as a group. It might be useful on the first few occasions that the technique is used to list some particular areas for the students to consider on the whiteboard so that they have a clear structure to follow.

GO TO ⋯⟩

Find a copy of a process review sheet on p29.

## The plenary

This stage of the exercise is an opportunity for students to share their experiences. Again, it should be as student-led as possible. Each group should be given the opportunity to present both their solution, and the reasoning behind their solution. It should also be possible for the other groups to question them about their work. Possible solutions might be written up on the board, and the main ideas behind them added. The students could then be asked to vote for the solution that they think is the wisest, and could be asked to discuss this in a follow-up piece of written work.

It is crucial, however, that as well as discussing the content, the process through which the solution was arrived at is also carefully and fully considered. This meta-level discussion will make explicit the thought and group processes involved and, through the use of a reflective diary or log, the ideas can be revisited the next time the technique is used, to help develop skills further and more directly.

It would also be useful to get the students to reflect on the idea of 'act local, think global', ie that the choices they make as individuals can have much greater consequences than they are immediately aware. Planetary stewardship can be seen to mean that we need to make wise choices at the individual level.

## Timings

It is vital that the students have a clear opportunity to discuss and consider both the content and the process involved in making a wise decision. For this reason students should not be made to reach conclusions quickly. An exercise such as this should be taught over a full two lessons (of approximately one hour each).

**Geography**

**Case Study 1**

*This dilemma asks the students to consider what they value most about the environment, and also exposes them to the reality of intractable dilemmas, where any decision will lead to major drawbacks.*

You work for a local council in the Yorkshire Dales. You have received an application from a mining company to develop an area of limestone moor land into a quarry. The application also states that the mining company would like to build a cement works as part of the site.

The local area has been hit hard by foot and mouth disease only a few years ago, and the closure of a factory in the local town. As a result local unemployment is very high. This has led to local young people moving away, and the sale of a number of houses to city-based professionals, who only use them in the holidays and at weekends. This has led to a number of local shops closing down.

However, the site is partially located in an area of recognised local beauty, and preliminary reports suggest that if the application were to go ahead it would have a very negative impact on local wild plants and animals. The site would also be in full view of several of the local villages.

What is your verdict?

## Introducing the dilemma

Having settled the group with some form of photo-orientated 'odd-one-out' exercise, it is time to begin the dilemma-based lesson. To begin with, the information given on p21 could be introduced on the whiteboard, and on copied sheets for the students. The dilemma should be read through and the students asked to spend a few minutes quietly considering the main pieces of information they have been given. Once this has been reflected upon, the students should then be invited to build a simple list or mind map on the board that highlights the key points. In this case, this might well include issues of environmental quality and conservation, but also issues of economic development and social change (for example, the loss of young people from the area). It would also be a good idea, in the context of this case study, to introduce other initial resources to 'ground' student thinking. For example, they might be given some photos and an OS map extract of an area that has a quarry, and the dilemma can therefore be given added pertinence by locating it within a real and specified place.

## Developing wisdom in groups

GO TO ⋯⟶

The roles are given on p7.

Having explicitly introduced some of the factors that might play a major part in the students' deliberation, split them up into small groups to discuss the issues and to attempt to develop a wise solution. If the exercise is being taught for the first time, or where there is little experience of the technique, the teacher might want to ask students to allocate themselves various roles to facilitate the work of the group. However, if students have used this technique before, it might be better to allow them to organise themselves. Each group is given an opportunity to use each of the Webs in turn to help scaffold their discussion. In this case study, some of the pertinent questions to highlight for students might include:

### The Think Web

- What makes this a dilemma?
- What are the key issues that might influence a solution?
- How many solutions can we find?

### The Me Web

- How would the main character feel?

### The Others Web

- Who else is mentioned in the dilemma?
- Is there anyone else who might be affected, but who isn't specifically mentioned?

### The Community Web

- What would happen in the long term to the local population?

This process should be used to allow the group to agree on a solution that they believe to be the wisest.

## Reflection on the process

GO TO ⋯⟶

Find a copy of a process review sheet on p29.

The group, having made their choice, should then be given an opportunity to reflect on the process they have been through. What is important here is that students have the chance to think through their own experience, and that of the group, properly. It is tempting to move through this element of the exercise quickly, but it is through this meta-cognitive discussion that the process of making wise choices has a real chance to develop. Therefore, students should fill in the process review sheet individually, and then come back together to discuss their work as a group. It might be useful on the first few occasions that the technique is used to list some particular areas for the students to consider on the whiteboard so that they have a clear structure to follow.

## The plenary

This stage of the exercise is an opportunity for students to share their experiences. Again, it should be as student-led as possible. Each group should be given the opportunity to present both their solution, and the reasoning behind their solution. It should also be possible for the other groups to question them about their work. Possible solutions might be written up on the board, and the main ideas behind them added. The students could then be asked to vote for the solution that they think is the wisest, and could be asked to discuss this in a follow-up piece of written work.

It is crucial, however, that as well as discussing the content, the process through which the solution was arrived at is also carefully and fully considered. This meta-level discussion will make explicit the thought and group processes involved and, through the use of a reflective diary or log, the ideas can be revisited the next time the technique is used, to help develop skills further and more directly.

## Timings

It is vital that the students have a clear opportunity to discuss and consider both the content and the process involved in making a wise decision. For this reason students should not be made to reach conclusions quickly. An exercise such as this should be taught over a full two lessons (of approximately one hour each).

# Personalising dilemmas

The use of dilemmas is very much context driven – they will suit a certain group at a certain time and in a certain way. Therefore, whilst it is important to build a bank of 'generic' examples, the best dilemmas are those developed by teachers to suit their own context. In this section, we provide some ideas on how dilemmas can be made to work for teachers and their students.

GO TO ⋯⟫

For a consideration of how to develop your own dilemmas see Section 2, p77.

Some of the main questions that teachers need to ask themselves in considering and personalising their use of dilemmas include:

- *What are the prior learning and experiences of the students?*
- *Which schemes of work and the elements embedded within them offer the best opportunities for the consideration of dilemmas?*
- *Where within a scheme of work would the dilemma(s) most easily sit?*
- *Is there really a dilemma to be used?*
- *What will the focus of the dilemma be?*
- *How can the outcome of a dilemma-based exercise be used?*
- *How will a debrief allow for greater understanding?*
- *How does the context of the group, and perhaps the school, play a role?*

*Analysis kills spontaneity. The grain once ground into flour, springs and germinates no more*

Henri Amiel

## What are the prior learning and experiences of the students?

It is important to ensure that the dilemma is based on students' prior learning and experiences. It is very easy to develop abstract ideas that have the academic potential to stretch and excite us but that are beyond the immediate understanding of the students. Therefore, we need to ensure that we develop dilemmas that are not too mundane or easy to reach a consensus on, but that, at the same time, do not baffle the students.

GO TO ⋯⟫

For further consideration of how to develop dilemmas which engage at the level of the student, see Section 3, p125.

## Which schemes of work and the elements embedded within them offer the best opportunities for the consideration of dilemmas?

When starting out with dilemmas, it may be possible to use resources that already exist. For example, many textbooks have decision-making exercises, or pose questions in a particular way that asks for a personal response from the students – this, with little (or perhaps no) effort, can be rephrased to give a simple dilemma some focus. Some schemes of work offer themselves to this form of reflection more readily than others – identify them and start from there.

## Where within a scheme of work would the dilemma(s) most easily sit?

Dilemmas can be used in many different ways, but a good way to get started is to think of them as an ignition exercise – allowing the students free range to consider an issue defined in general terms without the baggage of knowledge to impede their creativity and flexibility of thought. This will then lead to a more critical and original approach to the subsequent work.

## Is there really a dilemma to be used?

When first using this technique it is important that the dilemmas are clear-cut and understandable from both the viewpoint of the teacher and the students. It is important not to 'force' dilemmas, which might end up being either contrived or over-complex. It is better to try out a few clear opportunities that use obvious dilemmas so that students have the chance to understand the ambiguous nature of the exercise with which they are involved.

## What will the focus of the dilemma be?

The Webs of Meaning offer many different perspectives on a single dilemma. In some cases, you might decide that all of the questions contained in the Webs are important, leading to a greater and sustained use of the tool. However, at other times it might be considered important to use the technique to debate and reflect on specific and well-constrained areas.

## How can the outcome of a dilemma-based exercise be used?

We need to have a clear idea of how the ideas generated through the use of the dilemma will be used to deepen and extend students' understanding. This means that there needs to be a clear idea of how the outcomes will be used to greatest effect.

## How will a debrief allow for deeper understanding?

The debrief in any thinking-related exercise is crucial and the teacher needs to give careful consideration to what they want to focus on when debriefing the ideas and perceptions developed by the students. This will, to a degree, be aligned with the elements of the Web of Meaning that have been used, but will also require consideration of opportunities for taking the specific and extending them to the general, etc. For example, it might be helpful to ask a question such as 'How does this dilemma relate to things going on in the world today?' or 'Could anyone think of another event in history that seems to be similar in important ways to this dilemma.

## How does the context of the group, and perhaps the school, play a role?

As with prior learning and experience, the context of the group and the school are important – does the school/class environment present opportunities or barriers? What are they? How will they affect the dynamics of the exercise?

# Example from Geography, Case Study 1

**Geography** | **Case Study 1**

*This dilemma asks the students to consider what they value most about the environment, and also exposes them to the reality of intractable dilemmas, where any decision will lead to major drawbacks.*

You work for a local council in the Yorkshire Dales. You have received an application from a mining company to develop an area of limestone moor land into a quarry. The application also states that the mining company would like to build a cement works as part of the site.

The local area has been hit hard by foot and mouth disease only a few years ago, and the closure of a factory in the local town. As a result local unemployment is very high. This has led to local young people moving away, and the sale of a number of houses to city-based professionals, who only use them in the holidays and at weekends. This has led to a number of local shops closing down.

However, the site is partially located in an area of recognised local beauty, and preliminary reports suggest that if the application were to go ahead it would have a very negative impact on local wild plants and animals. The site would also be in full view of several of the local villages.

What is your verdict?

## Community Focus

This dilemma could be used to focus on the range of effects that a quarry development might have on different people and communities. Therefore, rather than using the whole Web of Meaning, the teacher might focus the attention of learners on the community element only.

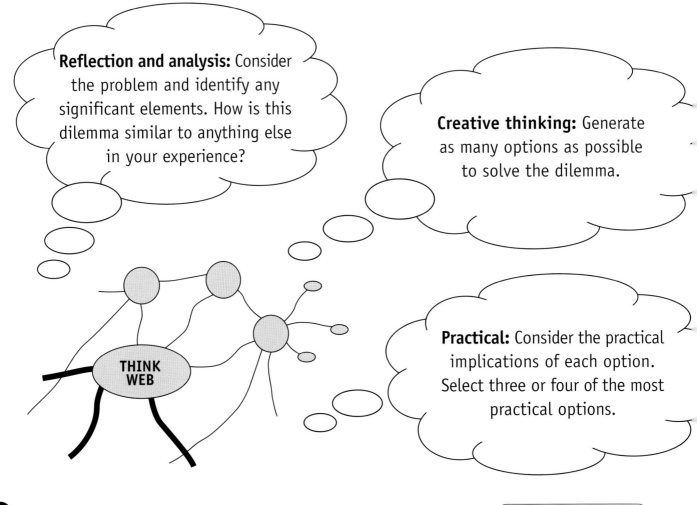

**Reflection and analysis:** Consider the problem and identify any significant elements. How is this dilemma similar to anything else in your experience?

**Creative thinking:** Generate as many options as possible to solve the dilemma.

**Practical:** Consider the practical implications of each option. Select three or four of the most practical options.

THINK WEB

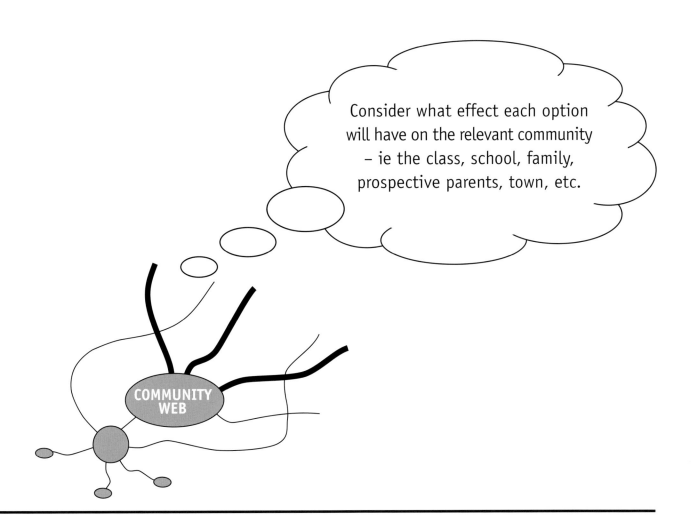

Consider what effect each option will have on the relevant community – ie the class, school, family, prospective parents, town, etc.

COMMUNITY WEB

## Thought Focus
An alternative approach could be used to focus students' attention on creating original solutions – thereby turning the task into more of a problem-solving and decision-making exercise.

# Beyond dilemmas – encouraging students to reflect on and apply their learning from a dilemma

At the conclusion of the dilemma-based learning group enquiry, there should be a chance for reflection and review of the process undertaken. Whilst this is easily squeezed out of a lesson – especially if the dilemmas have generated passionate discussion – this process review stage is potentially the most useful part of the dilemma-based learning experience. It provides a bridge from a particular dilemma to more generalised learning-to-learn skills and dispositions, which can impact on other areas of the curriculum. For this reason, 5-10 minutes at the end of the lesson should be protected for this purpose.

There may be a tendency, especially in the first few enquiries, for students to become emotionally attached to – or defensive about – their own ideas. This should be addressed over time, because it is a barrier to true enquiry. In a true enquiry, students are striving to find the 'truth' rather than merely to convince or to persuade. This tendency to identify with one's own views or suggestions is best explored openly at this process-review stage, rather than during the dilemma-based learning session itself.

The emphasis in this plenary session should be on how well the group worked together, and on metacognitive reflection – ie members reflecting on *how* they thought and contributed to the process. Each member of the group should take it in turns to say how he or she felt about the way they worked together. They should be invited to reflect on their contributions and thinking (a hard task), not to attribute blame to other group members (much easier). Key questions include:

- How do you feel now that the enquiry is over?
- Do you think you worked together to find the best/wisest solution?
- Are you happy with the final choice?
- Did you listen well and learn from each other?
- Did you build on each other's ideas or did you defend your own, even though it might not have been the 'wisest' solution?
- Are you pleased with your contributions?
- What skills did you use to address this dilemma? (eg the ability to listen, reflect, accept criticism of my views, persuade others, etc)
- What skills do you need to develop or work on?
- What contribution from other group members did you especially appreciate? (Ensure that each group member is appreciated for something.)
- How might you do things differently next time? Why?

Invite each member of the group to complete three short reflective statements for him or herself. These could be completed in exercise books, learning logs or a pro-forma:

- What I did well in this lesson was...
- What I could do better next time is...
- What I learned from doing this lesson is...

These statements can provide the teacher with helpful formative information about the students' learning, and should be dated and logged in an appropriate form.

It may also be helpful for the group as a whole to complete a group review record (see p29).

## PROCESS REVIEW RECORD: HOW WELL DID WE WORK AS A GROUP?

Group name:

| Level of work | Group criteria | ✓/✗ |
|---|---|---|
| 4 | Everyone contributed and expressed his or her ideas. | |
| | We worked together, cooperated and compromised. | |
| | We learned from each other when we disagreed. | |
| | We listened to each other's points of view. | |
| | We clarified and paraphrased what each other was saying, and showed empathy. | |
| 3 | We reached agreements through arguing and debate. | |
| | We sometimes clarified and paraphrased what each other was saying. | |
| | We sometimes strayed from the task. | |
| | Some members of the group remained silent or didn't join in. | |
| 2 | We were often off-task. | |
| | We rushed to complete the task. | |
| | We argued and upset each other. | |
| | Some of us felt our ideas were ignored. | |
| 1 | We did not stay on-task. | |
| | Some of us were not interested in the exercise. | |
| | We fell out about our ideas. | |
| 0 | Our group was chaotic. | |
| | We did not finish. | |
| | Put-downs were used in our group. | |
| | Some of us left the group. | |
| | Some of us complained about having to join in. | |

# Dilemma-based learning beyond the classroom – development of children in a wider context within school

The Every Child Matters agenda was implemented in the 2004 Children's Act and, as a result, services for children aligned their work to achieve five outcomes for children. These were: stay safe, be healthy, enjoy and achieve, make a positive contribution and achieve economic wellbeing.

Schools were charged with ensuring that the five outcomes were at the core of their work and they needed to show how they would achieve all of the outcomes and not just those that related directly to standards.

There are two complementary ways for schools to deliver the five outcomes. Firstly, by building a learning environment in which children have access to healthy food, appropriate exercise and remain safe and happy and, secondly, by teaching a curriculum designed to develop students' cognitive, social and emotional skills, values, dispositions and abilities, so that they can continue to meet the five outcomes throughout their lives. There are many ways of describing and classifying this generic set of skills – for example the National Curriculum provides a list of five thinking skills (information processing, reasoning, evaluation, creative thinking and enquiry).

*Excellence and Enjoyment: Learning and Teaching in the Primary Years (Primary National Strategy)* and *Leading in Learning: Developing Skills at Key Stage 3 (Secondary Strategy)* both outline thinking skills and their sub-skills. The Primary Strategy materials recognise that an effective school also promotes the social and emotional aspects of learning and have developed more comprehensive resources to support their development. Social and Emotional Aspects of Learning (SEAL) for Secondary Schools provides materials to support schools wishing to support learners with the development of social and emotional skills. This provides some example materials for Year 7 but encourages schools to develop their own unique approaches. Table 1 on p31 outlines the range of skills being promoted.

Young people live in a highly complex social and technological world. They need to be able to integrate cognitive and affective aspects of learning if they are to have a chance of effectively meeting the five outcomes. Unlike other approaches, dilemma-based learning explicitly encourages the integration of social, emotional and cognitive aspects of learning and their application to complex and conflicting contexts or dilemmas.

In practical terms, how might school curriculum planners use dilemma-based learning to plan the delivery of the five outcomes? The Webs of Meaning are inextricably linked with the skills outlined in Table 1. The idea is very simple but its impact is multi-layered and complex and its impact can permeate throughout a school. Consider that a school teaches in three ways: by what it teaches, by how it teaches and by the kind of place it is. The approach suggested in this book supports the explicit learning of the range of thinking skills and social and emotional skills – for example, those taken from Strategy documents in Table 1 .

In a dilemma-based learning lesson the role of the teacher/facilitator is to ensure that these skills are acquired, practised and extended through the mediation of the questions associated with each of the Webs. When students apply the Webs within the classroom they are provided with an opportunity to explore and develop their own understandings and meanings using the very skills, dispositions and abilities being explored. This means that the Webs of Meaning are both the tool that facilitates learning and the content of that learning. Furthermore, the process of using the Webs has the capacity to change the class climate and culture. Learners create the climate for learning by developing these skills and the climate itself is changed.

Let us consider the specific dilemma, climate change, and how this might be used in the classroom. The purpose will be for the students to reach an understanding about the

**Thinking, social and emotional skills identified and included in Secondary National Strategy materials**

# Thinking skills

**Information processing**

Locate and collect relevant information

Sort and classify

Sequence

Compare and contrast

Analyse part/whole relationships

**Reasoning**

Give reasons for opinions and actions

Draw inferences and make deductions

Explain what they think

Make informed judgments and decisions

**Enquiry**

Ask relevant questions

Pose and define problems

Plan what to do and how to research

Predict outcomes and anticipate consequences

Test conclusions and improve ideas

**Creative thinking**

Generate and extend ideas

Suggest hypotheses

Apply imagination

Look for alternative innovative outcomes

**Evaluation**

Evaluate information

Judge the value of what they read, hear and do

Develop criteria for judging the value of work or ideas

# Social and emotional skills

**Self-awareness**

Knowing myself

Understanding my feelings

**Managing my feelings**

Managing my expression of emotions

Changing uncomfortable feelings and increasing pleasant feelings

**Motivation**

Working towards goals

Persistence, resilience and optimism

Evaluation and review

**Empathy**

Understanding the thoughts and feelings of others

Valuing and supporting others

**Social skills**

Building and maintaining relationships

Belonging to groups

Solving problems, including interpersonal ones

## A framework of personal, learning and thinking skills 11-19 in England

### Independent enquirers

*Focus:*

Young people process and evaluate information in their investigations, planning what to do and how to go about it. They take informed and well-reasoned decisions, recognising that others have different beliefs and attitudes.

Young people:

- identify questions to answer and problems to resolve
- plan and carry out research, appreciating the consequences of decisions
- explore issues, events or problems from different perspectives
- analyse and evaluate information, judging its relevance and value
- consider the influence of circumstances, beliefs and feelings on decisions and events
- support conclusions, using reasoned arguments and evidence

### Creative thinkers

*Focus:*

Young people think creatively by generating and exploring ideas, making original connections. They try different ways to tackle a problem, working with others to find imaginative solutions and outcomes that are of value.

Young people:

- generate ideas and explore possibilities
- ask questions to extend their thinking
- connect their own and others' ideas and experiences in inventive ways
- question their own and others' assumptions
- try out alternatives or new solutions and follow ideas through
- adapt ideas as circumstances change

### Reflective learners

*Focus:*

Young people evaluate their strengths and limitations, setting themselves realistic goals with criteria for success. They monitor their own performance and progress, inviting feedback from others and making changes to further their learning.

Young people:

- assess themselves and others, identifying opportunities and achievements
- set goals with success criteria for their development and work
- review progress, acting on the outcomes
- invite feedback and deal positively with praise, setbacks and criticism
- evaluate experiences and learning to inform future progress
- communicate their learning in relevant ways for different audiences

## A framework of personal, learning and thinking skills 11-19 in England *Continued*

### Team workers

*Focus:*

Young people work confidently with others, adapting to different contexts and taking responsibility for their own part. They listen to and take account of different views. They form collaborative relationships, resolving issues to reach agreed outcomes.

Young people:

- collaborate with others to work towards common goals
- reach agreements, managing discussions to achieve results
- adapt behaviour to suit different roles and situations
- show fairness and consideration to others
- take responsibility, showing confidence in themselves and their contribution
- provide constructive support and feedback to others

### Self-managers

*Focus:*

Young people organise themselves, showing personal responsibility, initiative, creativity and enterprise with a commitment to learning and self-improvement. They actively embrace change, responding positively to new priorities, coping with challenges and looking for opportunities.

Young people:

- seek out challenges or new responsibilities and show flexibility when priorities change
- work towards goals, showing initiative, commitment and perseverance
- organise time and resources, prioritising actions
- anticipate, take and manage risks
- deal with competing pressures, including personal and work-related demands
- respond positively to change, seeking advice and support when needed
- express and manage emotions clearly

### Effective participators

*Focus:*

Young people actively engage with issues that affect them and those around them. They play a full part in the life of their school, college, workplace or wider community by taking responsible action to bring improvements for others as well as themselves.

Young people:

- discuss issues of concern, seeking resolution where needed
- present a persuasive case for action
- propose practical ways forward, breaking these down into manageable steps
- identify improvements that would benefit others as well as themselves
- try to influence others, negotiating and balancing diverse views to reach workable solutions
- act as an advocate for views and beliefs that may differ from their own

© Qualifications and Curriculum Authority

relationship between climate change and energy production *and* to learn thinking, social and emotional skills. Within the introduction to the lesson, the teacher/facilitator will review what skills, dispositions and abilities will be used and how this will be done. For example, he or she will make this learning explicit by eliciting ideas from the students about the effective use of the thinking skills and questions to be used in the Think Web, the social skills used within the Others and Community Web and the emotional skills used within the Me Web. In the lesson plenary, not only will learning about climate change and energy production be reviewed but students will be encouraged to reflect upon how they have used and developed their thinking, social and emotional skills in the process.

Throughout the lesson, students will use the Webs of Meaning to discover more about the issues surrounding climate change within a collaborative quest to reach the 'best' solution to the dilemma. As they do this, the questions on the Webs encourage them to explore their needs and feelings, the needs and feelings of others and to use the skills of enquiry, reasoning, problem-solving and creative thinking. These will be practiced implicitly within the learning process.

A lesson using the Webs of Meaning requires a distinctive learning environment. The layout of the classroom will need to be conducive to collaborative enquiry, the relationships will be of mutual trust and respect and the students will be leaders in their own learning. This learning environment provides opportunities for students to learn about themselves as social, emotional and thinking people. Just being in an effective dilemma-based learning classroom is designed to promote reflective, social and emotional learning.

# Reflecting and planning for dilemma-based learning

This section is intended to support those individuals who have tried some dilemma-based ideas in their classrooms, and want to consider both the initial level of success encountered and potential ways of taking the process forward.

## Initial reflections

If you have tried some of the dilemmas contained in this first section, or have decided to create some of your own using them as a template, consider some of the following questions:

- Who did you try the approach with?
- How successful was it?
- What was the reaction of the students?
- What do you feel they have gained from the experience?
- How did you use the Webs of Meaning to framework the students' thinking?
- How did the experience fit into the wider context of the work of the students at the time?
- Would you do anything differently next time?

## Developing the concept of Webs of Meaning further

This section has outlined the basic approach that can be used with dilemma-based learning. However, there is much more that can be developed within this approach. The main foci highlighted here include:

GO TO ⋯⟩

For an explanation of the 'spanner' see p77.

- the use of a 'spanner' to alter the context of the dilemma and cause cognitive conflict (Section 2)
- the use of dilemma-based learning to encourage students to consider the moral and ethical foundations of their thinking (Section 3)
- the use of Socratic questioning to encourage deep and critical discussion among students (Section 2)
- how dilemma-based learning can be used beyond the classroom as a tool for creative thinking and dilemma solutions within the wider school context (Sections 2 and 3).

---

### Table of example basic dilemmas

**Examples of basic history dilemmas**

| | | |
|---|---|---|
| Example 1 | The Peasants' Revolt | p36 |
| Example 2 | Industrial migration | p38 |
| Example 3 | The Holocaust | p40 |
| Example 4 | The Doomsday Book | p42 |

**Examples of basic religious education dilemmas**

| | | |
|---|---|---|
| Example 1 | The Good Samaritan | p44 |
| Example 2 | Making ethical decisions | p46 |
| Example 3 | Honesty | p48 |
| Example 4 | Justice | p50 |

**Examples of basic geography dilemmas**

| | | |
|---|---|---|
| Example 1 | Migration in Less Economically Developed Countries | p52 |
| Example 2 | Traffic worries | p54 |
| Example 3 | Ecological footprints | p56 |
| Example 4 | Introducing globalisation | p58 |

---

# Examples of basic history dilemmas

## The Peasants' Revolt

### Example 1

You are a newly crowned monarch, aged just 14. The times in your country are dangerous, and there are peasants rampaging through the streets of your capital. The Chancellor and the Archbishop have both been murdered by the mob.

The mob's leader is angry that the peasants have been heavily taxed, are not free to do as they wish and have to spend some of their time working for the nobility. He is demanding that all men are made free, and that the Church is forced to give up its huge ownership of land, so that the peasants can settle on it and call it their own.

You and your advisors must decide what to do.

## The Peasants' Revolt

Example 1

 **Background**

This dilemma considers the options facing Richard II at the time of the Revolt. Obviously there is an interesting issue to be considered here in terms of how the nobility and royalty regarded their subjects. This is an opportunity to discuss such issues – are they thinking like modern citizens in a democratic country, as opposed to a 14th-century king?

 **Context**

This dilemma provides a useful introduction to studying the Peasants' Revolt. It could be used as a first exercise, to introduce students to the main issues of the event, or to help them to understand the different moral and social beliefs of the period.

 **Focus**

This exercise is focused on personal reactions to basic information about an event. It also asks students to develop an ability to look at information from different perspectives to their own, as a 21st-century citizen. It also asks them to consider their own implicit points of view and reactions to a situation.

 **Webs**

All of the Webs would be useful in this exercise. However, if this is to be a brief exercise, particular focus could be given to the:
- Think Web
- Others Web
- Community Web

 **Questions**

This exercise engages students in personal reflection once they have completed the exercise. They may want to consider:
- What assumptions did I/we make about the information given to me/us?
- Why did the people involved have very different perspectives on the Revolt?

 **Following up**

Follow-up work could develop in many directions. One possible direction is:
- Ask students to research what happened to end the Revolt.

## Industrial migration

**Example 2**

It is early autumn, the leaves are falling from the trees in the lane as you trudge, hands stuffed in pockets, towards the inn. Work in the fields is now a memory of late summer, the harvest has been completed and stored. You now have five mouths to feed, with Milly having been born in the spring. Money is so tight, and the loom stands idle in the corner of the cottage. Over the past three years you've received less and less weaving piecework.

The inn is always near empty during the week. Your ale tastes good. After a little while, a face you recognise from some years ago appears at the bar. After buying a drink, the person comes over.

'John is that you?'

'Yes,' you reply.

'Hello, don't you recognise me? It's Luke.'

'Of course, I thought I recognised you. I thought you had gone to the city?'

'I have. I'm back for a couple of days, my father died and we buried him yesterday. I'm back to the city tomorrow.'

'Well, what's it like?'

'Hard. The pay isn't great, but it's steady. It allows us to rent a couple of clean rooms in a tenement, and there is food on the table and coal in the grate. You should come with your family, they need weavers, and there would be work for the wife and your children if they wanted it.'

This gets you thinking – is it a tempting offer?

*Chris Kington Publishing*

## Industrial migration

**Example 2**

###  Background

This dilemma allows students to understand the difficult choices that many people had to make in deciding whether to persevere in rural areas, or to migrate to the city. It highlights some of the factors responsible for pushing people to make one decision or the other.

###  Context

This dilemma is useful as part of a wider consideration of migration and the historical growth of cities. Used at the beginning of a unit of work on urban areas in the 19th century, or the period's economic history, it would help to develop background issues.

###  Focus

This exercise is focused on the difficult decisions that individuals had to make in deciding whether to move to urban areas or remain in rural areas as low paid labourers.

###  Webs

All of the Webs would be useful in this exercise. However, if this is to be a brief exercise, particular focus could be given to the:
• Think Web
• Me Web
• Others Web

###  Questions

This exercise engages students in personal reflection once they have completed the exercise. They may want to consider:
• What assumptions did I/we make about the information given to me/us?
• To what extent did I/we take into account the possible views of others in the family?
• What solutions did we/I come up with? Would they be realistic for those involved?

###  Following up

Follow-up work could develop in many directions. Two possible directions are:
• Ask students to research the living conditions in cities in the mid-19th century.
• Ask students to research what had happened in rural areas that made these decisions so important.

## The Holocaust

Example 3

You are living in wartime France, in a small town approximately 40 miles north of Paris. You have been married to your partner for 15 years and have a successful job as the town's doctor, their only access to a free source of medical help if needed. You also have three children, a daughter (12 years old) and two sons (eight and five years old).

It is late November 1943, when a friend comes to see you late one evening, just as you have finished at your surgery. You know he has links with the Resistance. He tells you that he knows of a Jewish family that has managed to elude the German authorities, but needs to move to a new safe house. He tells you that you are respected not only by the local French population, but by the German authorities also. He also tells you that the family has nowhere else to go.

Will you shelter them?

*Chris Kington Publishing*

## The Holocaust

Example 3

###  Background

This dilemma develops student thinking about the risks faced by both Jewish families and those who attempted to help them.

###  Context

This dilemma is useful as part of a wider examination of the Holocaust. It could be used to set up further study regarding what might happen to the family if they are not taken in, or are discovered once they are in hiding.

###  Focus

This exercise is focused on personal reactions to difficult decisions that not only affect those in danger, but those who attempt to care for them. It asks students to think about the wider ramifications of single, important decisions.

###  Webs

All of the Webs would be useful in this exercise. However, if this is to be a brief exercise, particular focus could be given to the:
- Me Web
- Others Web
- Community Web
- Balance Web

###  Questions

This exercise engages students in personal reflection once they have completed the exercise. They may want to consider:
- What assumptions did I/we make about the information given to me/us?
- Who were the most important people to me/us in deciding what to do?
- What potential effect would any decision have on those around me/us and further afield?

###  Following up

Follow-up work could develop in many directions. Two possible directions are:
- Ask students to research what happened to Jewish families who were caught by the authorities.
- Why does the location of the village in Northern France potentially make a difference?

## The Doomsday Book

Example 4

Looking over the rooftops of London from the vantage point of your keep, you realise that your hold on your newly conquered country is precarious. Your expedition has been expensive, your nobles want to see reward for their support, and you need to gain taxes from the populace.

You have no clear administrative structure through which to rule your country. Your councillors want to know how these problems will be solved.

They await your orders.

# The Doomsday Book

Example 4

##  Background

This dilemma helps students understand why William decided to create the Doomsday Book.

##  Context

This dilemma introduces the Doomsday Book and the development of the feudal system.

##  Focus

This exercise gets students to think about how they would try to secure power. It highlights the fact that this can be done in ways other than by force.

##  Webs

All of the Webs would be useful in this exercise. However, if this is to be a brief exercise, particular focus could be given to the:
- Me Web
- Think Web
- Others Web

##  Questions

This exercise engages students in personal reflection once they have completed the exercise. They may want to consider:
- What assumptions did I/we make about the information given to me/us?
- What kinds of ideas did I/we develop, and did they all require the use of power or force?

##  Following up

Follow-up work could develop in many directions. Two possible directions are:
- Ask students to research the creation of the Doomsday Book and its contents.
- Ask students to reflect on the effect the Doomsday Book had on the feudal system.

# Examples of basic religious education dilemmas

**The Good Samaritan?**                          Example 1

It is late at night and you have just finished watching a new blockbuster at the local cinema. Having said goodbye to some friends, you start to walk home.

Your route includes a quick walk through a local shopping area. You have passed this way nearly every day for the past four years. On this occasion, however, a couple of the street lamps are not working and as you approach the parade of shops, some other teenagers pass you in the opposite direction, laughing and throwing a bag to each other.

As you turn the corner to the shops, you notice what looks like a tramp slumped in a doorway.

What do you do next?

## The Good Samaritan

**Example 1**

###  Background

This dilemma asks students to think about how they would react to someone in need, especially where their own safety is not totally assured. It also acts as an introduction to the story of the Good Samaritan.

###  Context

This dilemma introduces the issue of moral conduct and the reasoning behind helping others less fortunate than ourselves.

###  Focus

This exercise is focused on personal reactions to the plight of others. It enables students to consider their own prejudices, assumptions and ethics.

###  Webs

All of the Webs would be useful in this exercise. However, if this is to be a brief exercise, particular focus could be given to the:
- Me Web
- Others Web
- Think Web

###  Questions

This exercise engages students in personal reflection once they have completed the exercise. They may want to consider:
- What assumptions did I/we make about the information given to me/us?
- How would I/we hope others would react to us if we were in need?

###  Following up

Follow-up work could develop in many directions. One possible direction is:
- Ask students to read and reflect on the study of the Good Samaritan. What are its main messages and how does it remain relevant to us today?

## Making ethical decisions

Example 2

The sea is grey – it swells, huge wave crests crashing. You look out from your berth on the cruise ship – this hadn't been in the brochure. The ship is juddering and making terrible noises. Then it happens: a message comes over the intercom and all passengers are asked to make their way to the mustering stations. You collect one or two small things and then head for the nearest station. Once there, you are given a lifejacket and told to follow a route to the deck. Once there, you are helped into a lifeboat.

You are lowered into the sea, spray is stinging your eyes, and you see the ship begin to slip below the water. Within 10 minutes, you can see people all around your lifeboat, heads held above the water by their lifejackets, but shouting for help. Looking back into the lifeboat, you see that only a few seats are empty and you are low in the water.

What do you do?

*Chris Kington Publishing*

## Making ethical decisions

Example 2

###  Background

This dilemma asks students to consider a difficult ethical issue. They are safe in the lifeboat – those around them are likely to die, but are they willing to jeopardise their safety for the life of others? Is there a point at which helping others will be to the detriment of all?

###  Context

This dilemma introduces the issue of personal ethics and the complexity of making positive ethical decisions.

###  Focus

This exercise is focused on personal reactions to an insurmountable dilemma. How will students decide on their course of action, and can they accept that at times there is no right decision that suits everyone?

###  Webs

All of the Webs would be useful in this exercise. However, if this is to be a brief exercise, particular focus could be given to the:
• Me Web
• Others Web
• Think Web

###  Questions

This exercise engages students in personal reflection once they have completed the exercise. They may want to consider:
• What assumptions did I/we make about the information given to me/us?
• Was I/we happy with the decision I/we made?
• Could I/we be happy with the decision I/we made?

###  Following up

Follow-up work could develop in many directions. Two possible directions are:
• Ask students to research a case study of an event where no one decision can bring a totally positive conclusion. What decisions were made? Could they have been better? What does this tell us?
• Some philosophers tell us that the good of the many is always more important than the good of the few. Is this always the case?

**Honesty**　　　　　　　　　　　　　　　　　　　　**Example 3**

You are walking home through the snow after a hard day at school. Some boys, including that horrible Simon, have been punching you and hurling snowballs at you again. They never seem to get told off.

You are kicking the snow angrily when a kick reveals a patch of colour exposed in the snow. You stop and look. Reaching down, you pick up a wallet. Looking inside, you find two £10 notes. In the front is an address card – the wallet belongs to Simon.

What do you do?

**Honesty**  **Example 3**

 **Background**

This dilemma asks students to consider personal ethics and the extent to which these are affected by the way that others treat us.

 **Context**

This dilemma examines ethical behaviour, especially in terms of basic religious values.

**Focus**

This exercise is focused on the extent to which our ethical decision-making can be affected by our relationships with other people. Is it ethically sound to react negatively to someone because they have been nasty to us? Or should we be able to rise above this and be true to our own ethical beliefs?

 **Webs**

All of the Webs would be useful in this exercise. However, if this is to be a brief exercise, particular focus could be given to the:
• Me Web
• Others Web
• Balance Web

**Q Questions**

This exercise engages students in personal reflection once they have completed the exercise. They may want to consider:
• What perspectives other than my/our own have we taken into account?
• How will our/my decision affect others?

**Following up**

Follow-up work could develop in many directions. Two possible directions are:
• Ask students to reflect on their decision. How would they react if they found out that Simon's brothers bully him on a regular basis – would this alter their view?
• Ask students to reflect on their own beliefs regarding honesty. Should you always be honest, or is honesty tied to context?

**Justice**

**Example 4**

Two individuals have come before a court, one charged with murder and the other with manslaughter. The first is found guilty of the premeditated murder of another man, who had been close to the girlfriend of the accused.

The second is found guilty of the manslaughter of another customer at a nightclub. They had become involved in a fight, and the accused had punched the other man, who had fallen back, hitting his head on the ground. He died five days later in hospital.

Both men have killed a person.

What sentences do you, as the judge, hand down? Why?

[You can deliver any punishment you choose, including the death penalty]

## Justice

**Example 4**

###  Background

This dilemma develops the idea of the positioned perspectives that we all have when approaching a situation or story, The students are being asked to consider what they believe to be a fair punishment for wrongdoing.

###  Context

This dilemma introduces the issues of justice, punishment and ethical acts impacting on others. It might also be interesting to consider the media and the part they play in framing our beliefs about justice.

###  Focus

This exercise focuses on personal reactions to illegal acts. It also focuses on the reasoning behind the use of punishment. What purpose does punishment serve? Retribution, rehabilitation or isolation from society? Students need to consider these issues when deciding upon appropriate punishment.

###  Webs

All of the Webs would be useful in this exercise. However, if this is to be a brief exercise, particular focus could be given to the:
- Me Web
- Think Web
- Community Web
- Balance Web

###  Questions

This exercise engages students in personal reflection once they have completed the exercise. They may want to consider:
- What assumptions did I/we make about the information given to me/us?
- How did I/we decide on a suitable punishment?
- How did I/we arrive at our point of view?

###  Following up

Follow-up work could develop in many directions. Two possible directions are:
- Ask students to research the penalties for crimes in another country. Do they agree with them and, if so, why?
- Ask students to reflect on their own ethical beliefs regarding justice and punishment. Ask them to explain and to reason why their viewpoint is a fair one.

# Examples of basic geography dilemmas

## Migration in Less Economically Developed Countries — Example 1

Roberto lives in a small village approximately 100km from a large city in Brazil. He is 15 years old, and has great difficulty finding stable work. He sometimes works on local farms with his father, but the labour is very strenuous, and pays very little.

At home, he is one of the main wage-earners together with his three brothers and a sister. They earn enough to look after their younger brothers and sisters who are at elementary school, and to pay the rent on their small home.

Roberto has been sent a letter from a friend who moved to the city two years ago. He says that it is possible to find work there collecting scrap metal from a large municipal rubbish heap and that the rates of pay are good for those who can salvage a large amount of metal. He also tells Roberto that he can stay with him if he wants to join him.

Should he go?

## Migration in Less Economically Developed Countries — Example 1

###  Background

This dilemma considers the difficult decisions made by the poor in order to survive.

###  Context

This dilemma introduces the topic of migration in Less Economically Developed Countries (LEDCs). It provides an empathetic introduction to the issue of rural-urban migration.

###  Focus

This exercise focuses on the difficult decisions made by many people who live in LEDCs. It challenges students to consider the decisions that individuals need to take in deciding their future. Does Roberto stay where he is, just about ensuring survival for himself and his family? Does he go, with the negative effect that this might have at home, but with the possibility that, if he does well, he can send money home?

###  Webs

All of the Webs would be useful in this exercise. However, if this is to be a brief exercise, particular focus could be given to the:
- Me Web
- Others Web
- Community Web

###  Questions

This exercise engages students in personal reflection once they have completed the exercise. They may want to consider:
- What assumptions did I/we make about the information given to me/us?
- Which factors were most important in helping me/us to make a decision?
- Was there an obvious answer?

###  Following up

Follow-up work could develop in many directions. Two possible directions are:
- Ask students to consider Roberto's future and that of his family.
- Ask students to research the wider factors involved in population movement in LEDCs, and the consequent impact of this on both cities and rural areas.

## Traffic worries

Example 2

Three days ago a pupil at your school was knocked over by a car and was seriously injured. The accident happened at home time, and the car involved belonged to a parent who was picking up their children.

There is a lot of congestion in front of the school every day, often caused by parents who live less than a mile from the school. In a recent home-school letter, a poll showed that many parents do not want their children to walk to school, even though the area has a very low crime rate.

Is this situation sustainable?

## Traffic worries

Example 2

###  Background

This dilemma introduces the idea of sustainability at a local level, and the choices that we need to make if we are to improve our local environments.

###  Context

This dilemma introduces the concept of sustainability, as it couches many of the arguments in a local, familiar context. This can then be widened out to bring in larger, more abstract ideas and examples.

###  Focus

This exercise focuses on personal responsibility and considers the kind of environment that the students would like to see around their own school grounds. It also asks them to consider the issue of traffic and their own movement to and from school.

###  Webs

All of the Webs would be useful in this exercise. However, if this is to be a brief exercise, particular focus could be given to the:
• Me Web
• Balance Web
• Community Web

### Q Questions

This exercise engages students in personal reflection once they have completed the exercise. They may want to consider:
• What assumptions did I/we make about our own environment?
• Did I/we take account of the possible viewpoints of others?

###  Following up

Follow-up work could develop in many directions. Two possible directions are:
• Ask students to develop a campaign for their school that focuses on traffic calming and sustainability.
• Ask students to reflect on their own opinions regarding sustainability, and to research and assess an example of traffic-calming measures in an urban area.

## Ecological footprints

Example 3

You receive a leaflet through the door from an environmental group that outlines the impact of energy use on the environment. The leaflet links the use of energy to global warming, pollution and desertification.

It also suggests that the average person in the United Kingdom has a large 'ecological footprint' and that we must reduce this if we are to save the planet. Two simple solutions are suggested: turning off lights when you leave a room, and going outside and getting exercise, instead of using computers and televisions.

What do you think?

*Chris Kington Publishing*

## Ecological footprints

**Example 3**

###  Background

This dilemma examines the role of personal responsibility in reducing ecological footprints. This could mean reducing the consumption of things that we most enjoy – in the absence of other long-term alternatives. This dilemma is also about students thinking about issues in the long term.

###  Context

This dilemma introduces issues of sustainability and ethical decision-making/consumerism. It acts as a good starting point for debate.

###  Focus

This exercise looks at the long-term effects of personal decision-making. We are often good at making wise decisions that have a short-term impact, but we are less able to do this when the effects (both positive and negative) are a long way off.

###  Webs

All of the Webs would be useful in this exercise. However, if this is to be a brief exercise, particular focus could be given to the:
• Me Web
• Others Web
• Community Web
• Balance Web

###  Questions

This exercise engages students in personal reflection once they have completed the exercise. They may want to consider:
• What timescale was I/we working on when making my/our decision?
• Did I/we consider other people and communities when making my/our choice?

###  Following up

Follow-up work could develop in many directions. Two possible directions are:
• Ask students to research and calculate their own ecological footprint – there are a number of calculators for this on the internet.
• Ask students to reflect on the size of their ecological footprint in comparison to that of other people around the world. Is this a fair comparison?

## Introducing globalisation

Example 4

A new shoe shop has opened in your town and is advertising the launch of a new style of trainer, which has had great reviews on the internet and in a magazine that you read. The shop also sells some great T-shirts that you and your mates really like.

On the day that the trainers are to be launched, a small group of protestors hands out some information that claims that the people making the trainers and clothes earn 30p a day. The factories that make the stock are in South East Asia, so the air miles have a very negative impact on the environment.

What do you choose to do?

## Introducing globalisation

Example 4

###  Background

This dilemma develops the idea of positioned perspectives that we all have when considering controversial issues. Is the information that is handed out true? How can students assess this? If it is true how should they react?

###  Context

This dilemma introduces the topic of globalisation and the subjective perspectives many people take in relation to its development.

###  Focus

This exercise focuses on our personal reactions to globalisation. Many students are not very good at understanding the positioned views of those on both sides of the debate, and it is important that they develop a critical approach to the information they are given if they are to make wise and informed choices about their consumer patterns.

###  Webs

All of the Webs would be useful in this exercise. However, if this is to be a brief exercise, particular focus could be given to the:
- Me Web
- Balance Web
- Community Web

### Questions

This exercise engages students in personal reflection once they have completed the exercise. They may want to consider:
- What assumptions did I/we make about the information given to me/us?
- Did I/we believe the information given to me/us or did we question it?
- On what basis did I/we make my/our final choice?

###  Following up

Follow-up work could develop in many directions. Two possible directions are:
- Ask students to research both sides of an issue concerning a multinational company or globalisation. What are the opposing viewpoints and which do they subscribe to – and why?
- Ask students to reflect on their own ethical beliefs and whether they believe globalisation is a positive or negative force.

*Chris Kington Publishing*

# Developing complexity in dilemma-based learning

# Developing complexity in dilemma-based learning

Section 2 introduces further elements to the dilemma-based learning experience, including a greater focus on questioning, group work and developing your own dilemmas. This section is intended for those who might have tried a few basic dilemmas and want to take the approach further.

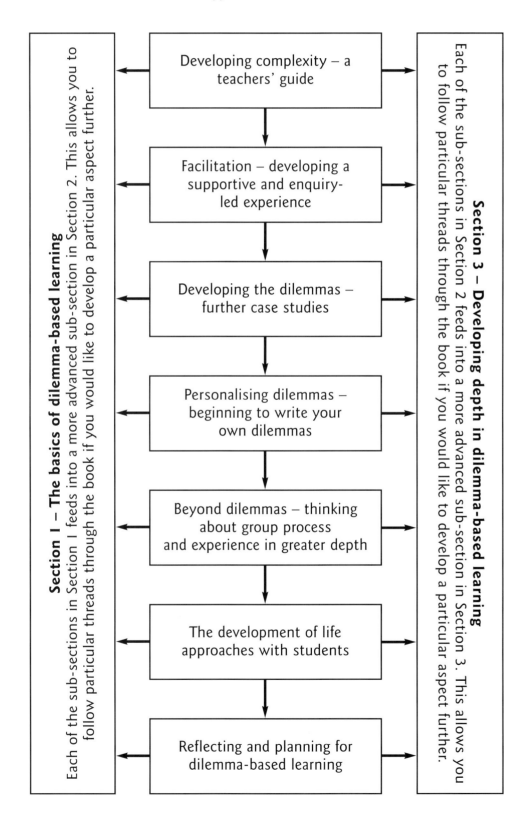

**Section I – The basics of dilemma-based learning**
Each of the sub-sections in Section I feeds into a more advanced sub-section in Section 2. This allows you to follow particular threads through the book if you would like to develop a particular aspect further.

Developing complexity – a teachers' guide

Facilitation – developing a supportive and enquiry-led experience

Developing the dilemmas – further case studies

Personalising dilemmas – beginning to write your own dilemmas

Beyond dilemmas – thinking about group process and experience in greater depth

The development of life approaches with students

Reflecting and planning for dilemma-based learning

**Section 3 – Developing depth in dilemma-based learning**
Each of the sub-sections in Section 2 feeds into a more advanced sub-section in Section 3. This allows you to follow particular threads through the book if you would like to develop a particular aspect further.

*Chris Kington Publishing*

# Developing complexity – a teachers' guide

> ## Aims
> - To discuss the role of questioning
> - To show you how to write your own dilemmas
> - To discuss the use of dilemma-based learning beyond the classroom

> ## Timings for training session
> - Considering the role of questioning in the classroom and how it can aid students' thinking (*20 minutes*)
> - Introducing the elements needed for a good dilemma (*20 minutes*)
> - Introducing ways in which dilemma-based learning might be used beyond the classroom (*20 minutes*)

## The role of questioning

In any technique where the purpose of the exercise is to help students to make decisions and develop arguments, there must be a focus on questioning. This skill is at the centre of dilemma-based learning, as we are essentially asking students to become wiser individuals and, as a consequence, we are asking them to ask questions of themselves.

**Q** **Consider the extent to which questioning is carried out by you (as opposed to your students) within your classrooms. Why does this balance exist?**

It is extremely important that students build a level of autonomy in their questioning within dilemma-based learning exercises. At first, they may not have the ability to do this, but your role is to model and mentor such approaches to help your students gain the skills necessary to do this.

**Q** **Try to list the various roles and reasons for questioning in a classroom. Once you have done this, turn to p65-67 and p77-78. Have you already considered these categories? How do they help students to develop their thinking?**

Focus on a small number of the questions to begin with and ensure that you use them in the classroom. After a while, add more to your repertoire and ask the students what questions they would like to use. At first you should model the questions, then mentor the students to use them, and finally you should withdraw to allow the students increasing autonomy. However, throughout the development of these skills you must ensure that their use and quality is included in any debrief of a dilemma.

## Elements of a good dilemma
## Let's use the dilemma we came across in Section 1:

*You know you are an excellent subject teacher. Your classes are well organised, and you genuinely enjoy the excitement of working with young people and trying out new ideas in the classroom. Your partner hates his/her job and would love to undertake a period of full-time study, leading to a change of career. If this were to happen, your family finances would be very tight.*

*A job is advertised at your school, and you know that you have a very good chance of getting it. However, it will take you out of the classroom, and burden you with greater management and administrative responsibilities. You'd enjoy these stresses much less than teaching – but the money would be good...*

**Q** Could we add anything to this dilemma to change its overall meaning? How about: 'the post is temporary for a year'. Does this alter the dynamics of the dilemma?

**Q** What makes this a good dilemma?

Once you have reflected on this question, turn to p77 to look at the elements of a good dilemma within a classroom setting.

## Dilemma-based learning beyond the classroom

Dilemma-based learning is not only an approach that can be used as an academic exercise. Indeed, it is at its best when it is used to solve real-life issues, and to help students to develop as people. The three main aspects that we are trying to develop by using this technique are:

- the emotional
- the social
- the behavioural.

**Q** Through the examples and the issues you have covered so far, how do you think dilemma-based learning develops the three traits given above?

**Q** Other than subject-based lessons, where and how might we use the technique to inform the work and decision-making of our students?

Turn to p81-82 to compare your ideas and read further.

# Facilitation – developing a supportive and enquiry-led experience

## Rationale for facilitation methods

The dilemma-based learning experience relies heavily on the development of students' process skills and learning dispositions in a group-learning context. For this reason, the outcome (ie the final decision with regard to a specific dilemma) is of less significance than such transferable skills and dispositions as creativity, critical reasoning, and empathic listening – all of which should be demonstrated by the students over the course of a dilemma-based learning lesson.

At its best, a dilemma-based learning lesson conforms to the definition of philosophy offered by the American psychologist William James: 'The dogged struggle to achieve clarity'. This 'dogged struggle' is a necessary and indispensable part of the move to clarity, and cannot and should not be rushed or in any other way abbreviated in the interests of time or the hasty achievement of 'lesson objectives'. The dilemma-based learning lesson includes devices that are designed specifically to *delay* resolution in the interests of a richer exploration of the core issues – eg such devices as the Webs of Meaning themselves, and the introduction of the 'spanner' at an appropriate point in the process. Dilemma-based learning lessons should be aimed, therefore, not at rapid progression to 'resolution', but at the careful teasing out of hidden meanings and creative possibilities, the eliciting of reasoned arguments and the clear articulation of the thinking behind students' suggestions, views and beliefs. This section explores the kind of questions, probes and other interventions (and indeed non-interventions!) that are designed to support the dilemma-based learning experience.

GO TO ⋯⟩

For a consideration of the development and use of the 'spanner' see p77.

## Use of process-praise and avoidance of performance-praise

In brief, it is important that we are slow to praise students for their abilities, their quick-thinking and their decisions. These outcomes have very little to do with the rationale and learning intentions of dilemma-based learning.

By contrast, we should be quick to praise evidence of process-skills – eg students' tenacity in the face of difficulties, their open-mindedness to others' competing views, their willingness to persuade and to be persuaded, etc. In this way we will, over time, communicate to students that what we value are the shifts in their thinking, communication and new insights (ie their *learning*), not their intelligence, speed of information-processing or capacity to second-guess the 'right' answer (ie their *performance*). This may be at variance with your students' usual experience of school, and this sense of dissonance can give rise to expressions of frustration or confusion, and you should be prepared for this. However, the principle of putting learning before performance has a strong pedigree in educational literature (most notably in the work of Professor Carol Dweck at Columbia University, Dr Chris Watkins at the Institute of Education, London, Professor Guy Claxton at Bristol University, and Professor Lauren Resnick at Pittsburgh University). This learning-first approach is known to promote the creation of mastery-oriented learners, who respond well to challenges, rather than performance-oriented knowers, who respond well to praise but who disintegrate in the face of challenges and difficulty (see Section 4, which relates to the theoretical underpinnings of the dilemma-based learning approach).

Teachers supporting dilemma-based learning lessons should avoid all comments that might be construed as implying judgement about anyone's abilities (including positive judgements), judgement about the 'right' or even a 'good' answer, or a belief that a contribution reflects that person's intelligence. These serve to locate the focus of the activity on the teacher's omniscience and authority, on the existence of a 'best' answer, and on students demonstrating their own abilities and prior knowledge, not their learning.

*Knowledge comes but wisdom lingers*
Alfred Lord Tennyson

Such unhelpful comments might include:

- 'That's not what I'd expect from someone of your ability...'
- 'That's a great idea...'
- 'You're brilliant – what a profound thought...'
- 'That's on the right track – well done!'
- 'I don't think that would work, would it?'

Instead, try to make more helpful comments that focus on the process of students' thinking and learning, their own judgements and their growing sense of agency and self-efficacy. Such process-observations could include:

- 'How do you feel having worked really hard at that?'
- 'You think now that you've been exploring a blind alley? Excellent! What have you learned from this, and where do you go from here?'
- 'Is there another way of looking at this?'
- 'Can you think of a situation where this wouldn't work?'
- 'You're stuck? Wonderful – you must have learned something to realise this! What do you do now?'

## Playing with process: probing for depth, connections and understanding

The following probes are designed to maintain focus on the students' thinking, and to resist or deflect entreaties for the teacher to resume responsibility for the thinking and learning. They can be used at any stage of the dilemma-based learning lesson, especially during whole-class or small-group consideration of the Webs of Meaning. The list is not exhaustive, but it aims to provide a framework for teachers new to the Webs of Meaning approach in particular, and to thinking skills approaches in general.

### Exploratory probes

- Why do you say that?
- Interesting – but what do you mean by...?
- Could you develop that thought a bit more?
- I'm not sure I understand that – could you provide an example?
- Could someone say what they thought when Safia suggested...?
- How would that help to...?
- Are you suggesting that...?
- Tell us again what you meant by...

### Probing for connections

- Is this similar to Jason's idea in any way?
- How does this relate to your original suggestion?
- Can you link this to the solution you mentioned earlier?
- Has anyone wondered if you've been down this track before?
- Does this help us? How?
- Is there a relationship between the two ideas?
- Where are the connections between these possible solutions?
- When?

 *Chris Kington Publishing*

## Probing for distinctions

- You dismissed Laura's idea earlier, but find this one acceptable. What's changed?
- How is this different from your first solution?
- Is this really a new idea? How is it different from what you said earlier?
- Are those views not compatible?
- Where do you two disagree?
- Suggest three ways in which your group's solution can be distinguished from that of the previous group.

# Developing the dilemmas – further case studies

## History
### Case Study 2

*This dilemma asks students to think about conscientious objectors and the laws passed during the First World War to force people to fight. As a Quaker (by convincement, and not by birthright), would Frank be willing to work as a translator and aid the war effort?*

---

You are jurors in a military tribunal that is hearing the case of a young man who refuses to join the army. It is late in 1916, after the passing of the Military Service Act that states all men between the ages of 18 and 41 must join the army. The man in question, Frank Delaney, has been refused a Certificate of Exemption, but has still not signed up to join a regiment.

He is short-sighted, and has lung problems, which often leave him short of breath. However, an army doctor has passed him as fit to see active service. His eldest brother is at the Front; two other brothers have already been killed in action.

His fiancé has called off their impending wedding, and has told him that she and her family want nothing more to do with him. His own family and neighbours have also ostracised him. Under the terms of the Act, unless he can give a clear and good reason for not joining (such as being outside the age limits for service, doing civilian work of 'national importance', etc) he can be forced to serve on the Front.

What do you decide?

---

Frank is a Quaker who attended Oxford University, where he gained a first-class degree in French and German. The Forces are short of good translators.

## Introducing the dilemma

Having settled the group with some form of starter, it is time to begin the dilemma-based lesson. To begin with, the information given on p68 could be introduced on the whiteboard, and on copied sheets for the students, although the 'spanner' would not be introduced at this time. The dilemma should be read through and the students asked to spend a few minutes quietly considering the main pieces of information they have been given. Once this has been reflected upon, the students should then be invited to build a simple list or mind map on the board that highlights the key points. In this case, the focus might be on the definition of a conscientious objector and the types of people who identified themselves as such.

## Developing wisdom in groups

Having explicitly introduced some of the factors that might play a major part in the students' deliberation, split them up into small groups to discuss the issues and to attempt to develop a wise solution. If the exercise is being taught for the first time, or where there is little experience of the technique, the teacher might want to ask students to allocate themselves various roles to facilitate the work of the group. However, if students have used this technique before, it might be better to allow them to organise themselves. Each group is given an opportunity to use each of the Webs in turn to help scaffold their discussion. In this case study, some of the pertinent questions to highlight for students might include:

GO TO ⋯⋗

The roles are given on p7.

### The Think Web
- What makes this a dilemma?
- What are the key issues that might influence a solution?
- How many solutions can we find?

### The Me Web
- How would the main character feel?

### The Others Web
- Who else is mentioned in the dilemma?
- Is there anyone else who might be affected, but who isn't specifically mentioned?

### The Community Web
- What would happen in the long term to the local population?

This process should be used to allow the group to agree on a solution that they believe to be the wisest.

## Introducing the 'spanner'

As you walk around the room, you will begin to sense that groups are coming to some level of agreement in their work, and will be close to choosing a solution to the dilemma. It is at this moment that you should introduce the 'spanner'. Read it to them and ask them to use the information provided to reconsider their decision. Give them time to deliberate properly on the new perspective that they have gained, and ensure that they integrate the ideas included into their discussions.

GO TO ⋯⋗

For an explanation of the 'spanner' see p77.

## Reflection on the process

The group, having made their choice, should then be given an opportunity to reflect on the process they have been through. What is important here is that students have the

GO TO ⋯⋡

Find a copy of a process
review sheet on p29.

chance to think through their own experience, and that of the group, properly. It is tempting to move through this element of the exercise quickly, but it is through this meta-cognitive discussion that the process of making wise choices has a real chance to develop. Therefore, students should fill in the process review sheet individually, and then come back together to discuss their work as a group. It might be useful on the first few occasions that the technique is used to list some particular areas for the students to consider on the whiteboard so that they have a clear structure to follow.

## The plenary

This stage of the exercise is an opportunity for students to share their experiences. Again, it should be as student-led as possible. Each group should be given the opportunity to present both their solution, and the reasoning behind their solution. It should also be possible for the other groups to question them about their work. Possible solutions might be written up on the board, and the main ideas behind them added. The students could then be asked to vote for the solution that they think is the wisest, and could be asked to discuss this in a follow-up piece of written work.

## Reflecting on the 'spanner'

Clear consideration should be given to the effect that the 'spanner' had on the group's thinking, and discussion should focus on how this altered their thinking (if at all) and why. This is an opportunity to demonstrate to students that often the choices that we make are complex, and we do not always have all of the facts available to us. As a consequence, students need to be able to work with cognitive conflict and ambiguity if they are to make wise choices.

It is crucial, however, that as well as discussing the content, the process through which the solution was arrived at is also carefully and fully considered. This meta-level discussion will make explicit the thought and group processes involved and, through the use of a reflective diary or log, the ideas can be revisited the next time the technique is used, to help develop skills further and more directly.

## Timings

It is vital that the students have a clear opportunity to discuss and consider both the content and the process involved in making a wise decision. For this reason students should not be made to reach conclusions quickly. An exercise such as this should be given a full two lessons (of approximately one hour each), or possibly even three, depending on the level of debate generated at each stage.

## Religious education

*This dilemma shows the difficulties in making decisions when relationships are not working. It also examines differing religious beliefs regarding the sanctity of marriage*

You have been in an unhappy marriage for the past 10 years. Your partner is a workaholic who spends little time at home, and while you have no evidence, there are rumours that your partner has been seeing other people.

You are in your mid-30s, with two young children (seven and four years old) and only see your partner briefly each day. A friend has suggested that, after several years of trying to make the relationship work, it is time to move on.

What do you think?

Both you and your partner are practising Roman Catholics.

## Introducing the dilemma

Having settled the group with some form of photo-orientated odd-one-out exercise, it is time to begin the dilemma-based lesson. To begin with, the information given on p71 could be introduced on the whiteboard, and on copied sheets for the students, although the 'spanner' would not be introduced at this time. The dilemma should be read through and the students asked to spend a few minutes quietly considering the main pieces of information they have been given. Once this has been reflected upon, the students should then be invited to build a simple list or mind map on the board that highlights the key points. In this case, these are issues surrounding the characteristics of a positive parnership, and the beliefs that different religions hold concerning the sanctity of marriage would be useful.

## Developing wisdom in groups

Having explicitly introduced some of the factors that might play a major part in the students' deliberation, split them up into small groups to discuss the issues and to attempt to develop a wise solution. If the exercise is being taught for the first time, or where there is little experience of the technique, the teacher might want to ask students to allocate themselves various roles to facilitate the work of the group. However, if students have used this technique before, it might be better to allow them to organise themselves. Each group is given an opportunity to use each of the Webs in turn to help scaffold their discussion. In this case study, some of the pertinent questions to highlight for students might include:

GO TO ⋯⫸

The roles are given on p7.

### The Think Web

- What makes this a dilemma?
- What are the key issues that might influence a solution?
- How many solutions can we find?

### The Me Web

- How would the main character feel?

### The Others Web

- Who else is mentioned in the dilemma?
- Is there anyone else who might be affected, but who isn't specifically mentioned?

### The Community Web

- What would happen in the long term to the local population?

This process should be used to allow the group to agree on a solution that they believe to be the wisest.

## Introducing the 'spanner'

GO TO ⋯⫸

For an explanation of the 'spanner' see p77.

As you walk around the room, you will begin to sense that groups are coming to some level of agreement in their work, and will be close to choosing a solution to the dilemma. It is at this moment that you should introduce the 'spanner'. Read it to them and asking them to use the information provided to reconsider their decision. Give them time to deliberate properly on the new perspective that they have gained, and ensure that they integrate the ideas included into their discussions.

## Reflection on the process

The group, having made their choice, should then be given an opportunity to reflect on the process they have been through. What is important here is that students have the

chance to think through their own experience, and that of the group, properly. It is tempting to move through this element of the exercise quickly, but it is through this meta-cognitive discussion that the process of making wise choices has a real chance to develop. Therefore, students should fill in the process review sheet individually, and then come back together to discuss their work as a group. It might be useful on the first few occasions that the technique is used to list some particular areas for the students to consider on the whiteboard so that they have a clear structure to follow.

GO TO ⋯⟩

Find a copy of a process review sheet on p29.

## The plenary

This stage of the exercise is an opportunity for students to share their experiences. Again, it should be as student-led as possible. Each group should be given the opportunity to present both their solution, and the reasoning behind their solution. It should also be possible for the other groups to question them about their work. Possible solutions might be written up on the board, and the main ideas behind them added. The students could then be asked to vote for the solution that they think is the wisest, and could be asked to discuss this in a follow-up piece of written work.

## Reflecting on the 'spanner'

Clear consideration should be given to the effect that the 'spanner' had on the group's thinking, and discussion should focus on how this altered their thinking (if at all) and why. This is an opportunity to demonstrate to students that often the choices that we make are complex, and we do not always have all of the facts available to us. As a consequence, students need to be able to work with cognitive conflict and ambiguity if they are to make wise choices.

It is crucial, however, that as well as discussing the content, the process through which the solution was arrived at is also carefully and fully considered. This meta-level discussion will make explicit the thought and group processes involved and, through the use of a reflective diary or log, the ideas can be revisited the next time the technique is used, to help develop skills further and more directly.

## Timings

It is vital that the students have a clear opportunity to discuss and consider both the content and the process involved in making a wise decision. For this reason students should not be made to reach conclusions quickly. An exercise such as this should be given a full two lessons (of approximately one hour each), or possibly even three, depending on the level of debate generated at each stage.

## Geography

*This dilemma highlights the environmental catastrophe enveloping places such as the Maldives. In a country that could see the first wholesale movement of its population as environmental refugees, the government faces a huge dilemma. The 'spanner' throws open the possibility that action thousands of miles away could have the greatest impact on the area.*

- Much of the Maldives lies less than 2m above sea level

- There are approximately 250,000 people living there

- Global warming is causing sea levels to rise

- What should the people on the Maldives do?

  - Nothing – allow the sea to claim some of their land, and live in ever-smaller spaces?

  - Spend money that they haven't got on building sea defences?

  - Leave – but which countries would take them as environmental refugees?

One way of lessening the effect and stopping rising sea levels would be to cut the amount of energy we use in places like the UK. If we alter our lives, could we help the people of the Maldives?

## Introducing the dilemma

Having settled the group with some form of photo-orientated odd-one-out exercise, it is time to begin the dilemma-based lesson. To begin with, the information given on p74 could be introduced on the whiteboard, and on copied sheets for the students, although the 'spanner' would not be introduced at this time. The dilemma should be read through and the students asked to spend a few minutes quietly considering the main pieces of information they have been given. Once this has been reflected upon, the students should then be invited to build a simple list or mind map on the board that highlights the key points. In this case, it might be useful to list some of the causes and effects of sea-level change.

## Developing wisdom in groups

Having explicitly introduced some of the factors that might play a major part in the students' deliberation, split them up into small groups to discuss the issues and to attempt to develop a wise solution. If the exercise is being taught for the first time, or where there is little experience of the technique, the teacher might want to ask students to allocate themselves various roles to facilitate the work of the group. However, if students have used this technique before, it might be better to allow them to organise themselves. Each group is given an opportunity to use each of the Webs in turn to help scaffold their discussion. In this case study, some of the pertinent questions to highlight for students might include:

GO TO ⋯⋗

The roles are given on p7.

### The Think Web

- What makes this a dilemma?
- What are the key issues that might influence a solution?
- How many solutions can we find?

### The Me Web

- How would the main character feel?

### The Others Web

- Who else is mentioned in the dilemma?
- Is there anyone else who might be affected, but who isn't specifically mentioned?

### The Community Web

- What would happen in the long term to the local population?

This process should be used to allow the group to agree on a solution that they believe to be the wisest.

## Introducing the 'spanner'

As you walk around the room, you will begin to sense that groups are coming to some level of agreement in their work, and will be close to choosing a solution to the dilemma. It is at this moment that you should introduce the 'spanner'. Read it to them and ask them to use the information provided to reconsider their decision. Give them time to deliberate properly on the new perspective that they have gained, and ensure that they integrate the ideas included into their discussions.

GO TO ⋯⋗

For an explanation of the 'spanner' see p77.

## Reflection on the process

The group, having made their choice, should then be given an opportunity to reflect on the process they have been through. What is important here is that students have the

GO TO ⋯⋗

Find a copy of a process review sheet on p29.

chance to think through their own experience, and that of the group, properly. It is tempting to move through this element of the exercise quickly, but it is through this meta-cognitive discussion that the process of making wise choices has a real chance to develop. Therefore, students should fill in the process review sheet individually, and then come back together to discuss their work as a group. It might be useful on the first few occasions that the technique is used to list some particular areas for the students to consider on the whiteboard so that they have a clear structure to follow.

## The plenary

This stage of the exercise is an opportunity for students to share their experiences. Again, it should be as student-led as possible. Each group should be given the opportunity to present both their solution, and the reasoning behind their solution. It should also be possible for the other groups to question them about their work. Possible solutions might be written up on the board, and the main ideas behind them added. The students could then be asked to vote for the solution that they think is the wisest, and could be asked to discuss this in a follow-up piece of written work.

## Reflecting on the 'spanner'

Clear consideration should be given to the effect that the 'spanner' had on the group's thinking, and discussion should focus on how this altered their thinking (if at all) and why. This is an opportunity to demonstrate to students that often the choices that we make are complex, and we do not always have all of the facts available to us. As a consequence, students need to be able to work with cognitive conflict and ambiguity if they are to make wise choices.

It is crucial, however, that as well as discussing the content, the process through which the solution was arrived at is also carefully and fully considered. This meta-level discussion will make explicit the thought and group processes involved and, through the use of a reflective diary or log, the ideas can be revisited the next time the technique is used, to help develop skills further and more directly.

## Timings

It is vital that the students have a clear opportunity to discuss and consider both the content and the process involved in making a wise decision. For this reason students should not be made to reach conclusions quickly. An exercise such as this should be given a full two lessons (of approximately one hour each), or possibly even three, depending on the level of debate generated at each stage.

*Chris Kington Publishing*

# Personalising dilemmas – beginning to write your own dilemmas

Once you have used some simple dilemmas, such as those that appear in Sections 1 and 2 of this book, you will want to start creating your own. A successful dilemma-based learning dilemma involves a number of parts that are essential if the exercise is to be successful.

## Someone must make a difficult choice

The central point of any dilemma is that the person involved needs to make a hard decision. A dilemma is, by definition, only a dilemma if there is no obvious solution to the problem.

## A starter 'hook'

There must be an interesting 'story' or focus if the person involved is to be 'hooked in' to the dilemma. This can be developed in a number of different ways. It might be an exciting topic, a subject that students are naturally drawn towards, or a focus that is current and relevant to the group involved. There is also no reasons why the hook – and indeed the wider dilemma – cannot be centred around a current local issue.

> *People are, if anything, more touchy about being thought silly than they are about being thought unjust*
>
> EB White

## Multiple options

This relates back to making a difficult decision. The dilemma needs to suggest a number of possible choices, as this is the process that will lead to students considering wise choices that occur from careful and reasoned consideration rather than gut reactions. The greater the number of potential solutions, the greater the degree of thought and discussion required by the students.

## No 'correct' answer

There should be no obvious correct answer to a dilemma, the whole point of a dilemma-based learning exercise is that students are required to, first of all, identify the different possibilities and, from this, discuss and develop solutions. If there is a correct answer, there can be no real dilemma.

## A degree of ambiguity, lack of detail

It is useful to keep the information that is given to students ambiguous. This leads to a greater number of possible solutions, and it also requires students to consider their assumptions about the information they have been given. Finally, it leaves the discussion open to interpretation and, as a consequence, a greater degree of debate is required by the students to come to a satisfactory conclusion.

## The 'spanner' – introducing cognitive conflict

Dilemmas such as those given in Section 1 are a simple starting point, and can work well in their own right. They fulfil the criteria given above and, as a way of developing skills with students, act as a good beginning. However, dilemma-based learning sessions can be used to delve much more deeply into dilemmas, probing the assumptions that we make about situations and highlighting the ambiguity and complexity of everyday situations. This can be done by using a 'spanner' (in other words, 'throwing a spanner into the works'). This is done by adding a layer of ambiguity to the dilemma, normally by turning it on its head. This can be seen in History, Case Study 2, on p68. The added information about Frank Delaney is intended to 'throw' the reasoned outcome that students have produced based on the

THE 'SPANNER'

information they were given in the main introduction to the exercise. An especially useful way of doing this is to allow students to spend 20-25 minutes using only the main information that you have given them. They use the Webs and discuss the outcome that they consider to be most appropriate. By listening to their discussions, it is possible to gauge the moment when most groups have almost made a decision. At this point, the 'spanner' is introduced, which clouds the issue once more and requires students to re-evaluate their ideas. This is a crucial part of a good dilemma, as it introduces cognitive conflict to the students, as they feel satisfied by their initial solutions, only to be shown a very different perspective that forces them to re-evaluate the information they have been given, and – potentially – the decision they have come to.

It is important that, in any debrief from the exercise, the use of the 'spanner' is discussed and considered. It should be stressed to students that the 'spanner' challenges them to accept that their answers might not always be fully informed, and that there is nothing wrong in re-evaluating their decision once they have a greater understanding of the facts and information. Ultimately, the 'spanner' is helping them to deal confidently with complexity and ambiguity.

## Exciting empathy and identification

Dilemmas are obviously best when they are exciting – either in terms of their usage in a dynamic part of a course, or in situations that are pertinent to the students themselves. This allows for a greater degree of empathy to be felt by the students. One way of developing this, even in remote historical periods, is through the personalisation of the situation. By looking at an issue from the perspective of a character, as in many of the exemplar dilemmas here, the students have a greater opportunity to empathise with that particular person. As a consequence, as the groups work through the Web questions, they can develop deeper insights into the issues at hand. Again, this can be used as a positive element of any debrief, as it allows for a wider discussion of how empathy can be used as a tool for helping us understand the perceptions and feelings of others as they might relate to us in real-life day-to-day dilemmas.

## Encouraging communication, discussion, debate

It is crucial in any Webs of Meaning experience that student groups are encouraged to communicate and debate. The Webs give a framework for this, and as outlined in Section 1, students can take on different roles to facilitate the efficient running of these debates. However, the central point is to get students discussing the issues. This can only happen in a safe and supportive climate, and it is therefore important to stress that these exercises have no one correct answer, and that all participants have a useful and positive role to play, as all views should be considered and discussed. Everything should be ruled in, nothing ruled out – initially.

## Access to resources – 'do-able' in the classroom

Finally, it is very important that the dilemma-based learning experience is achievable within the classroom context. As your confidence grows in using the technique, you may well decide to use other resources as part of the dilemma. For example, a dilemma centred on the extension of a limestone quarry might introduce maps, photos, data tables, etc as supporting information. In a history or religious education dilemma, video excerpts might be appropriate. However, in all cases, it is vital that any extra resources are easily and readily at hand. Once the debates have started, they should not be broken by pauses brought about by the need to search for information, or the correct part of a video tape. It might even be possible, with thorough preparation, to run a Webs of Meaning dilemma as an out-of-classroom exercise, with students finding extra information as part of their work in any given subject area.

# Beyond dilemmas – thinking about group process and experience in greater depth

## Group dynamics

If a dilemma-based learning experience is to work well, the dynamics of student groups needs to be carefully considered. Students need to be able to discuss ideas openly, and therefore should feel comfortable in their surroundings. It is important to foster a climate of mutual respect between students and emphasise that one of the main points of undertaking such an exercise is to listen and consider the ideas of others. Once the process has been completed a few times, the students should become more critically aware of factors that help groups to function well. As suggested in Section 1 (p29), a review record can be used to make the group explicitly aware of these factors.

Consideration of the task is important in deciding how and when the make-up of groups might be changed. Is it always appropriate to keep students in the same groups? This form of exercise is ideal for helping students to teach each other, and therefore consideration of differentiation and groupings can be both important and extremely useful. The main point of focus is how the experience can be made both positive and challenging. The group make-up may change constantly to reflect this.

## Questions and probes within groups

To help make wise decisions, students fundamentally need to be able to question and respond. The Webs of Meaning provide a core of questions that help students to framework their discussions, but they are not the only questions that may become important in developing debate. The teacher, whilst not the authoritarian figure of more traditional classrooms, cannot afford to sit quietly back and allow students to work wholly independently. They have a role to play in developing student questioning, and as such should constantly listen to the debates taking place in groups around the room. As a consequence, teachers can help to develop students'critical awareness by asking questions such as those given below:

### Probing for creativity

(helping students to consider new ideas, and to think more holistically and broadly)

- Who can suggest a way round this problem?
- Are there any new ideas we could introduce?
- Don't feel you have to think about the 'sensible' ways forward.
- Who feels differently? Why?
- Do you really all want to go with this?
- Is it possible that this isn't the best idea – just the one you're all stuck on?
- What would someone who disagreed with you say?
- If this doesn't work, what else could you do?
- Is there a contingency plan?

### Probing for critical reasoning

(developing the capacity of students to construct ideas and answers that can hold up to questioning and scrutiny)

- What's your evidence for saying that?
- I'd like to hear your reasons for that view.
- Does it follow that if... then...?

- Are we making any assumptions here?
- If we follow this line of reasoning to its logical conclusions, where would we be?
- Under what conditions would this not apply?
- So?
- And then...? What are the implications?
- How would you know that...?

### Metacognitive probes

(helping groups to become self-aware, and self-critical of the way in which they carry out the task)

- What kind of thinking are you doing here?
- Is there a core principle that you're working to here?
- How far have you come in your thinking?
- Whose suggestions have moved your thinking on? In what ways?
- Has your solution raised any new problems?
- Can you summarise this issue in the form of a question?

## Positive climate in the group

Children often find it difficult to separate their views from themselves, and as a result, if a member of a group offers a view that is unpopular with others, they can often feel slighted and become negative. It is important to develop in the groups an acceptance of ideas which should be considered in a positive way. Using some of the questions given above, the group should take ownership of the individual's idea, but then hold it up to analysis. At the same time, students should be aware that the critique of an idea is something quite different to a critique of themselves, a lesson many students are not taught. This is obviously something that can only develop over a period of time, and it is therefore important to discuss it not only as part of any debrief, but also as the occasions arise within group discussion.

## Listening as well as talking

It is obviously important that any group is well organised in terms of the debate and dialogue that emerges. It is increasingly true that students, even at secondary level, can find it difficult to listen to others. It is therefore important that groups use the dilemma-based learning experience as an opportunity to develop their listening skills, as the dilemmas that they face will only be resolved satisfactorily as a group if those taking part are willing to contribute in a positive and ordered way. Therefore, learning to listen, as well as explaining yourself clearly in a verbal sense, is crucial and, again, should be discussed openly with groups where required.

# The development of life approaches with students

Government-led initiatives to raise standards in schools, promote emotional health and wellbeing, prevent social exclusion and improve behaviour and attendance have led to increased interest in projects to enhance the social and emotional skills of learners. Although the purpose behind these initiatives is worthy, there are some dissenting voices expressing concern about teachers being encouraged to 'interfere in the emotional life' of children. The use of dilemma-based learning provides a way to balance the evident need for social and emotional learning (SEL) and counter the dangers of dictating and influencing when, how and what children might feel. During a lesson using dilemma-based learning the teacher acts as a facilitator, allowing the students to explore and discover their own social and emotional understanding in a structured and safe environment.

To be effective, dilemma-based learning should form part of a whole-school approach to promoting social, cognitive and emotional learning, which encompasses CPD approaches and school improvement processes. Ten attributes of effective programmes to promote social and emotional learning have been identified, as follows:

1. The programme will be grounded in theory and research and based on sound theories of child development.

2. It will teach children to apply SEL skills and ethical values in daily life through systematic instruction and the application of learning to everyday situations.

3. It will use diverse teaching methods to engage students.

4. It will provide developmentally and culturally appropriate instruction, including clearly specified learning objectives, for each Key Stage from preschool through secondary school. It will also emphasise cultural sensitivity and respect for diversity.

5. It will help schools coordinate and unify programmes that are often fragmented, offering a coherent, unifying framework to promote the positive social, emotional, and academic growth of all students.

6. It will enhance school performance by addressing the affective and social dimensions of academic learning.

7. It will involve families and communities as partners.

8. It ensures high-quality programme implementation by addressing factors that determine the long-term success or failure of school-based programmes. These include leadership, participation in programme planning by everyone involved, adequate time and resources, and alignment with school, local and national policies.

9. It offers well-planned professional development for all school personnel. This includes basic theoretical knowledge, modelling and practice of effective teaching methods, regular coaching, and constructive feedback from colleagues.

10. It incorporates continuing evaluation and improvement.

*Adapted from Collaborative for Academic, Social, and Emotional Learning (CASEL), University of Illinois at Chicago*

Dilemma-based learning can make a valuable contribution to whole-school approaches by providing a structure for thinking that allows for affective and cognitive learning together with academic and subject-based learning. The structure provided by Webs of Meaning ensures that social and emotional learning lies at the heart of subject-based study (see the contributions that dilemma-based learning can make to the new secondary curriculum, p164).

The purpose of social and emotional learning is to enhance students' skills, knowledge and understanding so that they can apply it to a range of situations outside the classroom. This will only take place with careful planning within a whole-school approach to ensure that learning acquired when using dilemma-based learning is applied beyond the safety of classroom discussions in humanities subjects to the real-life dilemmas that students will face in their daily lives. The following elements will be necessary to ensure that learning through subject-based dilemmas is maximised and applied spontaneously to decision-making by the learners in their lives outside school.

## Social dilemmas based on real-life experience

Dilemma-based learning should be used to explore social dilemmas that are grounded within the experiences of the students. These might be devised specifically, selected from newspapers or found within literature. Opportunities for this type of exploration might be provided within tutor time or PSHE. In this context students should be encouraged to draw upon their own experiences when exploring the Webs.

## Real social dilemmas

Students can be encouraged to provide their own 'dilemmas' for exploration using the Webs of Meaning. In most cases this might be posted anonymously within a 'worry' or 'dilemma' box. The teacher/facilitator should ensure that the dilemma is suitable for discussion and ensure the emotional safety of the student who donates the dilemma.

## Reflection after the event

> *Wisdom is the right use of knowledge. To know is not to be wise. Many men know a great deal, and are all the greater fools for it. There is no fool so great a fool as a knowing fool. But to know how to use knowledge is to have wisdom*
>
> Charles Haddon Spurgeon

Students are often unaware that they have a dilemma until it is too late and they are suffering the repercussions of their behaviour. Dilemma-based learning allows students to analyse the decision-making process after the event and come to their own understanding of how effective or 'wise' thinking could influence the outcome of their actions. Dilemma-based learning provides an ideal tool for pastoral staff when intervening in incidents of inappropriate behaviour.

## Student decision-making

Many schools are introducing school councils as important school decision-making bodies. At their best, they are part of a comprehensive decision-making system that draws on class-based councils. Dilemma-based learning can be used to support balanced decision-making.

Dilemma-based learning provides a structured approach to social and emotional learning across the curriculum as part of a whole-school development. The approach is most effective if students are supported to apply the learning in real life situations as part of planned provision and in response to real-life incidents as part of a whole-school initiative to promote social and emotional learning.

# Reflecting and planning for dilemma-based learning

This section is intended to support those individuals who have tried some of the more advanced ideas in their classrooms and beyond, and who want to reflect on their successes and areas for development.

## Initial reflections

If you developed your own dilemmas using some of the frameworks presented in this section, consider some of the following questions:

- Who did you try the approach with?
- How successful was it?
- What difference (if any) did the inclusion of a 'spanner' make?
- What do you feel they have gained from the experience?
- How did you incorporate ideas about questioning into your students' work?
- Did this make a difference to the level of debate entered into by your students?
- If you have used some of the techniques in situations other than humanities lessons, in what context did you use them?
- How successful was the experience?
- Would you do anything differently next time?

## Developing dilemma-based learning further

This section has outlined some of the more complex elements that can be used with dilemma-based learning. However, there is even more that can be developed within the approach. The main foci highlighted here include:

- the use of dilemma-based learning to encourage students to consider the moral and ethical foundations of their thinking (Section 3)
- the application of dilemma-based learning to difficult practical decision-making (Section 3)
- the ways in which dilemma-based learning can be used beyond the classroom as a tool for creative thinking and solving dilemmas within the wider school context (Section 3).

---

### Table of example 'spannered' dilemmas

**Examples of 'spannered' history dilemmas**

**Examples of 'spannered' religious education dilemmas**

**Examples of 'spannered' geography dilemmas**

---

# Examples of 'spannered' history dilemmas

## Elizabeth and the religious problem — Example 1

The year is 1559 and religion still plagues your thoughts as queen. The Anglican church continues to grow in confidence, whilst some of your loyal subjects, such as Lord Howard, wish to continue their observance of the Catholic faith. You know that religious strife still sweeps across much of mainland Europe, and that rebellion – or worse, civil war – would be disastrous for your still-precarious hold on the throne.

How will you unite the sides (if at all)?

*There is a sect in England called Puritans. These, following Calvin's teachings, reject all ancient ceremonies, they do not allow any organs or altars in their place of worship. They oppose any difference in rank among churchman, such as bishops, deans, etc.*

(Hentzner, 16th-century German traveller)

Will you placate this group?

## Elizabeth and the religious problem

Example 1

###  Background

This dilemma considers the often complex decisions we face. When confronted with a careful choice between two opposing courses of action, the decision can be difficult enough, but when a third element is added to the confusion, then it can become extremely difficult to find a successful resolution which will placate everyone – or do we accept that this is not always possible?

###  Context

This dilemma would act as a very good exercise as part of a wider consideration of the religious politics of the Tudor age. It might work well either as an introduction or an assessment of the understanding of the issues and decisions facing Elizabeth as she attempted to unite the country.

###  Focus

This exercise is focused on the complex decisions Elizabeth as queen was faced with if she was to unite and secure her own position on the throne. She, like many of us, faced very difficult circumstances at times, which required consideration of many different ideas and viewpoints, often held deeply by others. Hence, this is an opportunity to bridge the gap between issues in history and those which we face ourselves at a personal level.

###  Webs

All of the Webs would be useful in this exercise. However, if this is to be a brief exercise, particular focus could be given to the:
- Balance Web
- Others Web
- Community Web

### Q Questions

This exercise engages students in personal reflection once they have completed the exercise. They may want to consider:
- What were the difficulties with the options I/we originally developed?
- Did I change my point of view once I had all the facts?
- Why did I change my point of view?

###  Following up

Follow-up work could develop in many directions. Two possible directions are:
- Ask students to research the extent to which Elizabeth was actually successful in uniting the country.
- Ask students to reflect on how their own experiences of decision-making reflect those faced by Elizabeth.

## Dropping the atomic bomb

**Example 2**

After years spent on the Manhattan Project, you listen to the crackling of the aircraft's radio as it approaches its target. Every waking hour of your working life has been spent developing the technology that has led to this event.

Reports start to filter back from the area. There was a blinding light, a wave of heat and a wind that swept everything before it. Initial reports suggest that thousands have died. You find out weeks later that the official number is around 70,000, many of whom are women and children. In the meantime, another bomb has been dropped on another city, killing 36,000 people. Your work has helped to kill 100,000 people in less than a week.

If you had your time again, would you still dedicate yourself to this project?

Subsequent to your work, nuclear energy is developed, a way of cutting greenhouse gas emissions – although perhaps not totally safe in its own right. Some estimate that the lives of 1 million soldiers are saved by the dropping of the bombs. Nuclear technology also later becomes the focal point for a potential conflict between the USA and the Soviet Union. What unexpected consequences!

## Dropping the atomic bomb

**Example 2**

###  Background

This dilemma considers the wider outcomes (both positive and negative) of the Manhattan Project. We often make decisions based on their immediate impact and effects, but the 'spanner' in this dilemma is intended to move students away from this way of framing a decision to the wider and longer-term effects that their initial decision could have.

###  Context

This dilemma considers events at the end of the Second World War. It allows students to explore the ethics of the atomic bomb attacks and also the long-term effects of the Manhattan Project in arenas other than war, such as energy production and, later, geopolitics.

###  Focus

This exercise is focused on the timeframes over which we consider issues in our own lives. Often when we make decisions we do not consider the effects that don't seem relevant to us at the time.

###  Webs

All of the Webs would be useful in this exercise. However, if this is to be a brief exercise, particular focus could be given to the:
- Me Web
- Others Web
- Community Web
- Think Web

###  Questions

This exercise engages students in personal reflection once they have completed the exercise. They may want to consider:
- What impact did I/we initially believe our decision would have on both others and wider communities?
- Did I change my point of view once I had all the facts?
- Why did I change my point of view?

###  Following up

Follow-up work could develop in many directions. Two possible directions are:
- Ask students to research the immediate impact of the Manhattan Project, and compare it with its longer-term, less direct effects. As such, do they believe, on balance, that it was a good or bad thing?
- Ask students to reflect on their own viewpoints about the ethics of dropping the atomic bomb.

## Factory reform in the 19th century

### Example 3

You sit down to have your breakfast, like all mornings, but this turns out to be a special day. As you start your meal, a note is brought to you from your servant. You decide to open it and almost choke as you read its contents.

It is from a fellow Member of Parliament, who has written to let you know that you must be at the House of Commons in four days time, as the government has put forward a new Factory Reform Act. They want to restrict the time that children are allowed to work to six and a half hours each day. They say that this is necessary to keep children safe from the dangers of the factory workplace. You know that many of the families who send their children to work in local factories do so as they need their children to earn the extra money, otherwise they would struggle more than they already do. Also, where would the children go during the day when their parents are at work?

How will you vote?

You are a factory owner yourself, and have a record of seven infant deaths over the past year alone.

*Chris Kington Publishing*

## Factory reform in the 19th century

Example 3

###  Background

This dilemma examines the positioned viewpoints and the alien way in which sections of society thought about each other in a period different to that of the students. It also highlights the very utilitarian view that some have in make decisions which discounts any emotional perspective.

###  Context

This dilemma helps students to understand the positions and principles held in the 19th century about children. This could be done either at the start or the end of such a lesson to stimulate or develop ideas.

###  Focus

This exercise looks at the belief systems of people from a different age. Childhood was not seen then in the same way as it is now. Did people see the use of child labour as something wrong? It also asks students to consider the position of factory workers, who themselves may have relied on the wages obtained by their own children.

###  Webs

All of the Webs would be useful in this exercise. However, if this is to be a brief exercise, particular focus could be given to the:

- Think Web
- Me Web
- Community Web

###  Questions

This exercise engages students in personal reflection once they have completed the exercise. They may want to consider:

- In deciding on possible outcomes to what extent did I/we consider the status of the children involved?
- Did I change my point of view once I had all the facts?
- Why did I change my point of view?

###  Following up

Follow-up work could develop in many directions. Two possible directions are:

- Ask students to research the working conditions of children in the 19th century, and the extent to which factory laws affected working practices.
- Ask students to reflect on their own working lives, if they have them, and how different they are to those of children in the Victorian period. Do they believe that children should be able to work more today?

## The collapse of communism

**Example 4**

You stand in the study of the general secretary, finally you have the power held by other great politicians before you, Stalin, Brezhnev. However, as the first few days of your rule bring you information about your country that you have not had before, you begin to realise that there are problems. The economy is weak, with the quality of goods in decline, wheat production at a low, with the need to import millions of tonnes from the USA, and money is still further drained by your continued arms race with the USA. You also know the true cost of the loss of money and troops in Afghanistan.

People at home are becoming increasingly restless, even with the threat of the army and the KGB, and the opinions of dissidents across the world are more often heard at home.

How will you take your country forward?

A number of peripheral republics in the wider USSR are beginning to flex their power and demand greater autonomy, some being the richest republics in terms of natural resources. Your advisors tell you that the political confidence of these republics is due to the success of Solidarity in Poland.

## The collapse of communism

**Example 4**

 **Background**

This dilemma has been written to develop the complex and unstable situations which we can find ourselves in where any choice does not seem to be a good one. It perhaps requires us to think of creative and new ways to consider both the problem and the limitation of damage in a situation, rather than a solution that is entirely positive.

 **Context**

This dilemma examines events at the end of the Soviet Union. Before considering the policies of the country under Mikhail Gorbachev, students could complete the exercise to understand the complex situation in which he found himself.

 **Focus**

This exercise examines the choices facing Mikhail Gorbachev as he took power in the Soviet Union. The country faced problems that could not be resolved easily using the traditional approaches taken by those before him. He had to think in a new way and develop new ideas – with only partial success.

 **Webs**

All of the Webs would be useful in this exercise. However, if this is to be a brief exercise, particular focus could be given to the:
- Balance Web
- Others Web
- Community Web

**Q** **Questions**

This exercise engages students in personal reflection once they have completed the exercise. They may want to consider:
- How did I/we react to the complexity of the initial situation?
- Did I change my point of view once I had all the facts?
- Why did I change my point of view?

 **Following up**

Follow-up work could develop in many directions. Two possible directions are:
- Ask students to research the policies followed by Gorbachev, and how successful they appeared to be.
- Ask students to consider the extent to which Gorbachev was forced to follow the policies that he did.

# Examples of 'spannered' religious education dilemmas

**War**                                                                    **Example 1**

You call an emergency meeting of the government to discuss reports that have reached you concerning the development of a military threat in another country. This country has made threats towards you in the past and is now accusing your government of being extremists, only intent on ruling over others.

How do you respond?

_____

You are the president of a small central American country and the threat comes from the USA.

## War

Example 1

###  Background

This dilemma challenges the assumptions that we make when we do not have access to all the facts. This dilemma is ambiguous, as the students will often assume the country being threatened is their own. The 'spanner' is deliberately placed to challenge these assumptions.

###  Context

This dilemma is useful as part of a module of work on war and conflict, asking students to consider the different perspectives taken in a conflict by sides that believe that they are justified and right. Obviously, these are subjective positions.

###  Focus

This exercise shows the choices facing people when they consider conflict. Do people only need to be threatened to react in certain ways, or is there a need to develop greater understanding to avoid conflict? It also demonstrates that we can sometimes develop whole rationales with too little information, thereby making rash decisions.

###  Webs

All of the Webs would be useful in this exercise. However, if this is to be a brief exercise, particular focus could be given to the:
• Me Web
• Others Web
• Community Web

###  Questions

This exercise engages students in personal reflection once they have completed the exercise. They may want to consider:
• How did I/we react to the initial situation?
• Did I change my point of view once I had all the facts?
• Why did I change my point of view?

###  Following up

Follow-up work could develop in many directions. Two possible directions are:
• Ask students to research the arguments made for wars in the past and to consider to what extent these were based on an informed choice, or as the result of a reaction that had not been fully considered.
• Ask students to consider if war is ever justifiable, and whether there are any arguments that can be translated from this to conflict in our daily lives.

## Dilemmas about money

**Example 2**

You sit at your dining room table with your partner – you don't know what to think. You have twins, aged 17, and you have recently won £1,000 on the Lottery. You normally have just enough money to survive, but with this windfall you can make a difference to the life of one of your children. One son has done really well at school, through hard work and application. He is trying to get to a really good university, and you know that attending a school revision trip in the Easter holidays will really boost his chances. If your son does not go to university he may end up having to follow his father into the local factory – something neither of them want.

However, your other son has recently been diagnosed with a mental illness. Doctors believe that this has been made worse by his soft drugs habit. Unfortunately, a drug treatment that can help to stabilise him is not offered on the NHS. The money from the Lottery win would provide your son with this drug for 18 months.

What should you do?

Whilst you are considering what to do with your money, your boiler stops working. A friend who is a plumber gets it going again, but tells you it won't last more than three months. He can get you a new one at trade price, and will fit it for free, but it will cost £600.

*Chris Kington Publishing*

## Dilemmas about money

Example 2

###  Background

This dilemma enables students to recognise that the acquisition of money and its subsequent use are not always straightforward. In this case, the money that has been received can only help in a limited way. What is the best way of spending it?

###  Context

This dilemma is useful as part of a module of work on choice, money, and personal decision-making. It helps to develop the idea that while we want more money, do we ever have enough of it?

###  Focus

This exercise examines how we respond to difficult choices, and may also relate to personal ethics. However, do the students support the 'good' son, who already has a positive start ahead of him, or the 'bad' son, who has perhaps added to his own problems through lack of self-care. The 'spanner' then introduces the question as to whether the money is spent on everyone, but in a more mundane way.

###  Webs

All of the Webs would be useful in this exercise. However, if this is to be a brief exercise, particular focus could be given to the:
- Me Web
- Others Web
- Think Web

###  Questions

This exercise engages students in personal reflection once they have completed the exercise. They may want to consider:
- How did I/we react to the initial situation?
- Did I change my point of view once I had all the facts?
- Why did I change my point of view?

###  Following up

Follow-up work could develop in many directions. Two possible directions are:
- Ask students to reflect on their choice of action and why they felt it was appropriate.
- Ask students to consider how the two sons might have reacted to different decisions and compare this to the story of Cain and Abel.

## Abortion

## Example 3

You have recently been promoted to the position of government advisor on embryology and childbirth. A research project has been lodged with your authority that proposes a course of work that would eradicate specific genetic defects over the course of the next 50 years. However, to do this, testing would be required on a large but unspecified number of defective and healthy embryos. This process will lead to the termination of these embryos.

What do you advise the government to do?

---

While you are deliberating, a small research project is published from scientists in another country, where the government has decided to allow such embryo experiments to go ahead. They will no doubt patent the treatments they develop if they get there first, leaving your country, and others, to pay for the use of the new technologies. The politicians in your country are already asking questions.

*Chris Kington Publishing*

**Abortion**  **Example 3**

 **Background**

There is much debate about research into genetics, stem cells and the rights and wrongs of abortion. This dilemma asks students to consider their own ethical views and the extent to which these should/can be set against economics.

 **Context**

This dilemma introduces the ethics of abortion, and medical research, especially as medical research increasingly has to take economics into account. It would provide a clear line of subsequent enquiry concerning the morality of this complex area.

**Focus**

This exercise examines the choices facing those working in the medical sciences sector. It is difficult to ensure ethical standards while also considering what is useful both for future generations and economically driven research. However, what emphasis is afforded to the unborn embryo?

 **Webs**

All of the Webs would be useful in this exercise. However, if this is to be a brief exercise, particular focus could be given to the:
• Me Web
• Others Web
• Balance Web

**Q Questions**

This exercise engages students in personal reflection once they have completed the exercise. They may want to consider:
• How did I/we react to the complexity of the initial situation?
• Did I change my point of view once I had all the facts?
• Why did I change my point of view?

**Following up**

Follow-up work could develop in many directions. Two possible directions are:
• Ask students to research the present policies on stem cell and embryological research. Do they seem ethical?
• Ask students to consider the extent to which the needs of medical research outweigh ethical considerations regarding the rights of embryos.

## Environmental stewardship

### Example 4

Drivers passing through Everytown find it hard going. There's heavy congestion and the town is very polluted.

Plans are proposed to bypass the town with a new dual carriageway. The planned route goes through an area of open woodland that includes the habitat of a rare snail. This habitat will be destroyed if the plan goes ahead. However, the snail has two other recognised habitats close to other towns in the region.

At a council meeting local residents argue that the bypass is necessary for health and safety reasons. A local environmental group ask how many habitats can be lost before road expansion stops.

Do we need snails anyway?

As you debate the decision, it is found that of the two remaining snail habitats, one is scheduled to be levelled for a housing estate. Department of transport officials also identify your town as having the most unsustainable traffic system in the country.

*Chris Kington Publishing*

## Environmental stewardship

Example 4

###  Background

The media is increasingly preoccupied with the lifestyle decisions we make and the impact they have on our environment, eg global warming. To what extent should we accommodate the environment in our decision-making, or do we do whatever is easiest and most convenient for ourselves?

###  Context

This dilemma introduces the topic of environmental stewardship, throwing up a number of questions concerning our practical and ethical ties to the environment.

###  Focus

This exercise highlights the difficult ethical choices we make, and the long-term effects of these choices. If we make poor local decisions, can they be amplified over time in other places? Do we value things in other than financial terms?

###  Webs

All of the Webs would be useful in this exercise. However, if this is to be a brief exercise, particular focus could be given to the:
- Me Web
- Balance Web
- Community Web

### Q Questions

This exercise engages students in personal reflection once they have completed the exercise. They may want to consider:
- What factors were most important in deciding my/our decisions?
- Did I change my point of view once I had all the facts?
- Why did I change my point of view?

###  Following up

Follow-up work could develop in many directions. Two possible directions are:
- Ask students to consider their own personal values in relation to the decisions discussed. Are they willing to make choices that might inconvenience them if there is a positive reason to do so?
- Ask students to reflect on the extent to which the same choices are still relevant to us on a global scale.

# Examples of 'spannered' geography dilemmas

## Issues with resources

### Example 1

- The world population is growing.

- Many resources are finite – ie they will run out once they have been used.

- People in rich countries use more resources than people in poor countries. For example, each person in the UK uses the same amount of resources as 40 people living in India.

- As the world's population increases and resources run out, people will starve.

- You have been elected prime minister.

- Politicians know that people don't like to be told bad news, especially if they are telling people that they have to give up some of their possessions.

- At a world summit meeting, you have to give a speech to other world leaders, saying what you think the world should do about population and resources. What will you say?

Use the following to help you make your decision:

- How many different solutions can you think of?

- Choose three or four options from your list.

- List the different groups who will be affected by your decision.

- How will each of these groups be affected?

- What are your own views on the dilemma?

- What are the practical possible outcomes of your decision?

---

You are the prime minister of a very poor country in southern Africa.

## Issues with resources

Example 1

###  Background

This dilemma considers difficult political decisions that need to be taken when considering the use of finite resources and their distribution between countries of contrasting economic wealth.

###  Context

This dilemma introduces decision-making and resource use. It also highlights issues of inequality and globalisation.

###  Focus

This exercise encourages students to understand the difficulties that politicians face when making decisions that will adversely affect the lives of their citizens. By providing generalised information it also tests the assumptions made by students when considering information. They will assume and make decisions initially based on being 'British', an assumption clearly challenged by the spanner!

###  Webs

All of the Webs would be useful in this exercise. However, if this is to be a brief exercise, particular focus could be given to the:
- Me Web
- Others Web
- Community Web

###  Questions

This exercise engages students in personal reflection once they have completed the exercise. They may want to consider:
- How did I/we decide on an initial solution? What assumptions had I/we made at this time?
- Did I change my point of view once I had all the facts?
- Why did I change my point of view?

###  Following up

Follow-up work could develop in many directions. Two possible directions are:
- Ask students to research the differing resource use between More Economically Developed Countries and Less Economically Developed Countries. Is this situation fair?
- Ask students to consider the extent to which they would be willing to change their lifestyles (if at all) to achieve greater global equality of resources and how they would do this.

## Tourist impact in the Himalayas — Example 2

You live in a small village in the Himalayas. The slopes are steep, and you spend your time caring for and maintaining the terraces and retaining walls that give the slopes of the valley a staircase-like appearance. It is a hard life, but you manage to survive. Your health and that of your family are good, and with help from a small charity based in the United Kingdom, you have recently installed a micro-hydro system which has brought electricity to the village for the first time.

A representative from a tourist company visits you and talks to the elders of the village. He proposes the building of a trekkers' bunkhouse where tourists will stay, on their way to the higher peaks of the Himalayas. The local villagers will run the bunkhouse, and through the charges made to the tourists, will make a profit. Over a period of time, some of this profit will pay back the cost of the bunkhouse, and ownership will eventually transfer to the village.

The representative adds that the bunkhouse will be a full-time but seasonal job, which will employ many in the village. Also, if numbers are poor for the first two years, they will cease to use the bunkhouse on their tours, but the outstanding costs will still need to be paid.

What is the most positive choice for the village? Should you agree to the building of the bunkhouse?

---

Global trends in climate threaten to have a dramatic impact on the Himalayan landscape, with shrinking glaciers and greater rainfall making slopes more unstable, and also making the region less sustainable for tourism.

## Tourist impact in the Himalayas

**Example 2**

 ### Background

This example highlights the dilemmas that some people in poor parts of the world face when trying to secure their financial future. On one hand, tourism no doubt seems very attractive, but if this leaves fields unattended, is the future sustainable? However, as long as it lasts, tourism might be more profitable. But then again, there are the loans needed for development to consider.

 ### Context

This dilemma would act as a very good exercise as part of work on development, tourism and rural geographies by stimulating debate about a community's possible future.

 ### Focus

This exercise makes students aware of the tough decisions that people have to make in trying to secure their economic future. Development is a process that affects people at a personal level but, as the 'spanner' suggests, the changing global climate can affect the outcome of such decisions.

 ### Webs

All of the Webs would be useful in this exercise. However, if this is to be a brief exercise, particular focus could be given to the:
• Think Web
• Me Web
• Community Web

 ### Questions

This exercise engages students in personal reflection once they have completed the exercise. They may want to consider:
• Which factors were important in helping you decide your initial solution (ie before the 'spanner')?
• Did I change my point of view once I had all the facts?
• Why did I change my point of view?

 ### Following up

Follow-up work could develop in many directions. Two possible directions are:
• Ask students to research the impact of tourism on the Himalayas and the extent to which this can be viewed as a positive or negative thing.
• Ask students to reflect on the work of aid agencies in one part of the less economically developed world and the degree to which their work can be seen as sustainable.

## Coastal management

Example 3

An international report has stated that sea levels are estimated to rise by 50-90cm over the next 25 years. This has led to calculations that, along the stretch of coastline on which you live, the number of storm surges causing noticeable damage to the coastline – a mixture of cliffs, bays and beaches backed by sand dunes – will increase from three per year to eight per year with an associated increased erosion rate from an average loss of 50cm depth of coastline per year to approximately 80-90cm.

You have lived in your home for over 30 years, and love living only 500m from the sea. You can see out over the sea in the evenings while working in your office.

A newsletter from the district council asks you to return your views concerning the best course of action. They suggest that hard engineering solutions can be used, especially sea walls and revetments, but at great expense, leading to higher council tax bills. The main alternative is to use dredging and beach nourishment; this is less expensive, but will need to be used more often. Again there is a cost implication, which needs to be met by local populations to a degree.

The other option is to do nothing. You know that you could leave, and, for the time being, you would be able to sell your house (something that could become more difficult in the future).

Which option do you go for?

---

You are a local councillor for the area, and represent the Green Party.

Chris Kington Publishing

## Coastal management

**Example 3**

###  Background

This dilemma outlines a classic geographical problem, ie how best to manage a shifting and increasingly unstable coastline. Students will need to consider the issue in the context of someone who lives in the area, and will thus have a personal attachment to it. This will obviously affect the options presented.

###  Context

This dilemma introduces the topic of coastal management. The technical detail can be explained in subsequent lessons.

###  Focus

This exercise demonstrates the choices facing local people and councils in trying to sustain coastal communities. Cost, environmental impact, and the personal preferences that people hold, often due to particular perspectives, are all important. The 'spanner' will force the students to take on a postioned response – an environmentalist who may want to save their home, but may also find that any form of intervention constitutes a moral problem.

###  Webs

All of the Webs would be useful in this exercise. However, if this is to be a brief exercise, particular focus could be given to the:
• Me Web
• Others Web
• Community Web

###  Questions

This exercise engages students in personal reflection once they have completed the exercise. They may want to consider:
• What factors did I/we find most important in making my/our initial decision?
• Did I change my point of view once I had all the facts?
• Why did I change my point of view?

###  Following up

Follow-up work could develop in many directions. Two possible directions are:
• Ask students to research a coastal management case study and the local protests/discussions included in resolving the situation.
• Ask students to consider the long-term effects of different types of coastal defence – are all coastal communities sustainable?

## Multinationals

**Example 4**

A new outlet of a large national superstore opens near your home, opposite a row of shops owned by locals. The shops have been there since the 1920s and offer a lot of the basics that aren't otherwise available unless you go right into the centre of town, or round the bypass to a large superstore – owned by the company that is opening its new store close to your home.

The prices at the new shop are known to be cheaper, and the choice seems greater in the new outlet. Soon after the store opens, one of the local shops closes down, a newsagent owned by the parents of one of your friends.

Who do you decide to shop with in future?

_____

The local newspaper publishes a news story that prices in other branches of the superstore have been raised once the local competition has gone. However, they do stock a magazine you couldn't find in the local shops beforehand.

## Multinationals

**Example 4**

 ### Background

This dilemma asks students to consider the effects of large chainstores/multinationals establishing themselves in direct competition with small local shops. Obviously, it is tempting, and often more economical, to use these stores, but have the students considered whether or not shops are solely about profit, or in some cases do they serve a community role? Does this matter?

 ### Context

This dilemma could be used in conjunction with work on commercial location, shopping, or as part of an introduction to a consideration of multinationals and globalisation. In each case, it would serve as a useful introduction to generate debate and enquiry-based questions.

 ### Focus

We often make economic decisions that are based in the short term, seeing low prices or convenience as crucial factors in making decisions. This dilemma highlights the social effects of local shops, which we may not consciously consider as consumers. This dilemma also asks of us whether short-term gains are sometimes counteracted by longer-term issues that have not been fully considered.

 ### Webs

All of the Webs would be useful in this exercise. However, if this is to be a brief exercise, particular focus could be given to the:
• Think Web
• Me Web
• Community Web

 ### Questions

This exercise engages students in personal reflection once they have completed the exercise. They may want to consider:
• How did I/we make my/our initial decision? What were we basing our thinking on?
• Did I change my point of view once I had all the facts?
• Why did I change my point of view?

 ### Following up

Follow-up work could develop in many directions. Two possible directions are:
• Ask students to research the influence of large companies on one consumer area which they are involved in, eg food, clothes, music, etc.
• Ask students to investigate the changing pattern of shops in their area and current consumer trends.

*Chris Kington Publishing*

# Developing depth in dilemma-based learning

# Developing depth in dilemma-based learning

Section 3 focuses on introducing extra elements to the dilemma-based learning experience, including a focus on ethics. This is intended for those who are confident in using dilemmas and want to take the approach further.

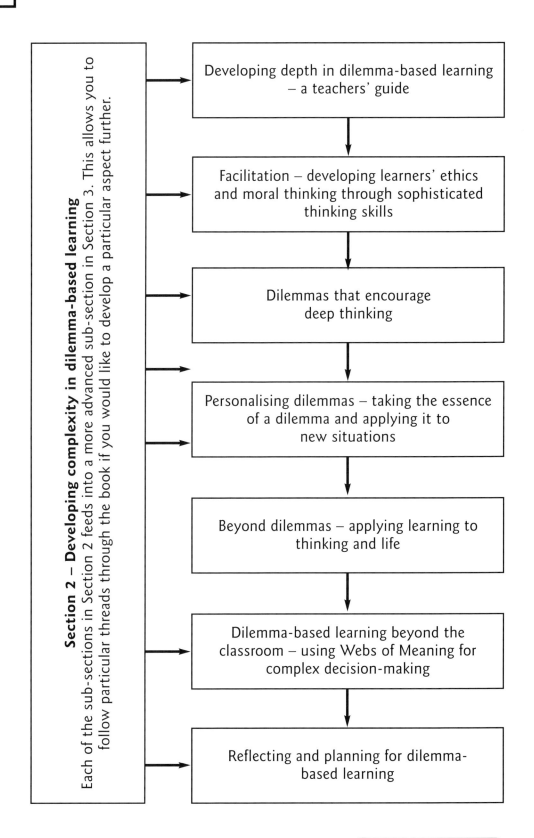

**Section 2 – Developing complexity in dilemma-based learning**
Each of the sub-sections in Section 2 feeds into a more advanced sub-section in Section 3. This allows you to follow particular threads through the book if you would like to develop a particular aspect further.

Developing depth in dilemma-based learning – a teachers' guide

Facilitation – developing learners' ethics and moral thinking through sophisticated thinking skills

Dilemmas that encourage deep thinking

Personalising dilemmas – taking the essence of a dilemma and applying it to new situations

Beyond dilemmas – applying learning to thinking and life

Dilemma-based learning beyond the classroom – using Webs of Meaning for complex decision-making

Reflecting and planning for dilemma-based learning

# Developing depth in dilemma-based learning – a teachers' guide

## Aims

- To discuss the importance of ethics
- To consider developing dilemmas that are taken from external sources

## Timings for training session

- Considering the role of ethics in making decisions about dilemmas
  (*30 minutes*)
- Considering the development of dilemmas form external sources (*30 minutes*)

## The role of ethics

In making decisions about dilemmas, we always see the potential validity of the solution from our own personal perspective, which in turn is the result of our own ethical standpoint. If we take the religious dilemma presented as Case Study 3, on p118:

*Your partner has been rushed into hospital having suffered from emphysema for some years. They are now unable to walk and even talking is difficult. They have to remain on bottled oxygen for much of the day. Doctors are finding it hard to stabilise your partner, who has already been resuscitated twice. Although your partner does seem somewhat better, they are in constant pain.*

*You have been told that your partner should be able to live for another four to five weeks, but that during that time they will have to be heavily sedated. Alternatively, the doctors are willing to withdraw treatment whilst keeping your partner comfortable.*

*They can't help you decide what to do on this occasion.*

 *You know that your partner has made a living will asking that, if they are in severe and terminal pain, they should be allowed to die. Your children have arrived at the hospital and want your partner's treatment to continue, but do not know about the living will.*

This dilemma allows us the opportunity to consider the ethical stance involved in such a situation.

**Q Consider or discuss what you believe to be the most ethical solution to this dilemma. Share your ideas, or try to develop alternative solutions. Is there only one possible solution?**

**Q Why might it be important to discuss these ethical ideas with students? What might they gain from such an experience?**

Once you have had a chance to discuss or consider these ideas, turn to p113.

## Development of dilemmas from external sources

It is often the case that we may want to use dilemma-based learning for curriculum/content purposes, and indeed, some of the dilemmas included here are written to that end. However, it is often the case that students will react more positively when dilemmas offer a more personal way in to a subject. Hence, we need to take the essence of an abstract dilemma and alter it to suit the lives of the students. Try one of the following:

**1.** Take a current news story

or

**2.** Use the Opium Wars example (History, Case Study 3, p115).

In either case, develop another dilemma that takes the essence of the story and position it in the students' local area and experience, while retaining the essential nature of the dilemma.

**Q Consider the advantages of altering a dilemma in this way. What will it add to your students' experience and the depth of their discussions?**

Once you have done this, turn to p125 for a more detailed examination of how you can alter events, dilemmas, etc in this way.

*Chris Kington Publishing*

# Facilitation – developing learners' ethics and moral thinking through sophisticated thinking skills

## Why ethics?

Ethics is the study of 'right conduct'. In other words it is a theory or system of moral values, and the moral choices that individuals make. As such, the vast majority of choices we make from day to day are informed by the moral beliefs we hold as individuals. This can be seen throughout this text as, if we take any of the dilemmas presented, they ask us to make some form of choice, but each choice is, at its foundation, a moral choice. For example, if we are considering whether or not we should bend, or even break, a law to gain a greater amount of political power, we are making a moral choice. We might be able to justify that it will be for the greater good of those living in the country – alternatively, we may decide that laws are there for the long-term benefit of the population and that to break them is wrong. In either case, the individual has made a moral choice.

Therefore, the dilemma-based learning method helps students become wiser individuals by not only asking them to make better and more informed choices through the use of a number of questions, but also by considering what they believe to be ethical choices. However, it is important that we help students to make decisions for themselves – we must not moralise and assume that our own moral compasses are superior to those of our students. They must be given time and space to discuss and consider these difficult ideas and questions for themselves.

> *Wisdom outweighs any wealth*
> Sophocles

## Developing personal ethics

Dilemma-based learning focuses on the development of wisdom, and much of this is achieved through interaction with others. As such it involves asking students to engage socially and understand the need to look further into the future to appreciate the consequences of actions. Ethics is a significant framework for helping them in this pursuit. The dilemma itself gives plenty of opportunity to discuss ideas from different perspectives, and also allows students to air and listen to different ideas from within the group. As discussed in Section 2, this requires them to listen to each other and understand that the views of others, whilst they might not agree with them, are still important and need to be considered. This relies on students suspending the usual confrontational debating style that is so prevalent. As such, this requires a reconfiguration of ethical stances by some individuals, who will need time and help to readjust to this new mode of enquiry.

## Considering the foundations of a decision

Decisions are normally made by weighing up evidence. However, one problem with this is that individuals often see evidence in different ways. A good example was a television advert for the *Guardian* newspaper that depicted a teenager pushing an elderly person in the street. The assumption we make from the evidence is that the teenager is mugging the person, or harming them in some way. However, a different camera angle then shows a piano slipping away from a crane tether and falling to the ground – above where the old person is standing.

This demonstrates that the perspectives we hold on an issue, and the morals that underpin this, fundamentally affect our understanding and view of that issue. As a consequence, we need to discuss students' morals and ethical ideas with them, to help them make wise choices and decisions.

## Debriefing on ethics

The trouble with any discussion of ethics within the classroom is that we can be accused of moralising. This is a real danger, and must be avoided at all costs. To moralise to students is to attempt to force them to have a single perspective on an issue, *our* perspective.

When explicitly involving ethics in a dilemma-based learning exercise, a positive structure is as follows:

- Complete the dilemma as outlined in Sections 1 and 2.
- Having completed the dilemma, and discussed the students' decisions, insert the ethical element (see the case studies in this section).
- It is important to set guidelines. An ethical debate does not mean that 'anything goes'. It should be made clear that racist comments, etc are unacceptable and that in any follow-up work such comments will be penalised. Depending on the nature of the exercise or school, other guidelines may also be put in place.
- Beyond this baseline expectation, we must allow students to make their own choices and express themselves, to do otherwise shows that we are not really interested in what they have to say.
- In any discussion and follow-up work, make it clear that you are looking for clear, reasoned ideas and beliefs that can be backed up with evidence. When feeding back to students, ask searching questions of their ideas, and what evidence they can produce to support their views.

By following this basic structure, the students have the opportunity to express their ideas, but they are also being challenged and held to account, so that they have to question and consider their own ethical foundations.

*Passive acceptance of the teacher's wisdom is easy to most boys and girls. It involves no effort of independent thought, and seems rational because the teacher knows more than his pupils; it is moreover the way to win the favour of the teacher unless he is a very exceptional man. Yet the habit of passive acceptance is a disastrous one in later life. It causes man to seek and to accept a leader, and to accept as a leader whoever is established in that position*

Bertrand Russell

# Dilemmas that encourage deep thinking – case studies

**History**                                                                 **Case Study 3**

*This dilemma asks students to consider the role of unsavoury facts in the history of all countries. Also, it asks students to consider if we should treat ALL people the same regardless of their nationality.*

You are governor general of India and have received a letter, via Queen Victoria, from a Chinese diplomat called Lin Tse-hsu. He has asked that you stop the East India Company from shipping opium (the base ingredient of heroin, which can be smoked in its own right) into China. Your government has already made the shipping of opium to England, and the use of opium as a drug, illegal. However, the East India Company trades the opium for tea, china porcelain, and silk, all of which are highly prized in England, and all of which bring a huge amount of revenue to the country. The East India Company is obviously not happy to stop its production of opium in India, as it is a major source of profit for the company. However, it is also known that the drug has caused huge social problems in the large cities of China.

What do you tell your advisors to do?

Lin Tse-hsu has threatened to arrest and imprison English traders suspected of dealing in opium within China, regardless of your decision, and to sink any boats entering Chinese waters that might be carrying opium.

- What was your final decision?
- List the factors that made you decide as you did.
- Why did you think that these factors were important?
- Does the history of our country as the world's biggest supplier of drugs in the 19th century make it more difficult for us to tackle international drugs trafficking now?

Write a summary that explains your decision and the reasons behind it. Try to explain what led you to think that these reasons are so important.

## Introducing the dilemma

Having settled the group with some form of photo-orientated odd-one-out exercise, it is time to begin the dilemma-based lesson. To begin with, the information given on p115 could be introduced on the whiteboard, and on copied sheets for the students, although the 'spanner' would not be introduced at this time. The dilemma should be read through and the students asked to spend a few minutes quietly considering the main pieces of information they have been given. Once this has been reflected upon, the students should then be invited to build a simple list or mind map on the board that highlights the key points. In this case, a consideration of the importance of trade to the British empire and its people might be useful, including the products and commodities that we now see as part of our own culture (tea, etc).

## Developing wisdom in groups

Having explicitly introduced some of the factors that might play a major part in the students' deliberation, split them up into small groups to discuss the issues and to attempt to develop a wise solution. If the exercise is being taught for the first time, or where there is little experience of the technique, the teacher might want to ask students to allocate themselves various roles to facilitate the work of the group. However, if students have used this technique before, it might be better to allow them to organise themselves. Each group is given an opportunity to use each of the Webs in turn to help scaffold their discussion. In this case study, some of the pertinent questions to highlight for students might include:

GO TO ⋯⫶

The roles are given on p7.

### The Think Web

- What makes this a dilemma?
- What are the key issues that might influence a solution?
- How many solutions can we find?

### The Me Web

- How would the main character feel?

### The Others Web

- Who else is mentioned in the dilemma?
- Is there anyone else who might be affected, but who isn't specifically mentioned?

### The Community Web

- What would happen in the long term to the local population?

This process should be used to allow the group to agree on a solution that they believe to be the wisest.

## Introducing the 'spanner'

GO TO ⋯⫶

For an explanation of the 'spanner' see p77.
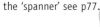

As you walk around the room, you will begin to sense that groups are coming to some level of agreement in their work, and will be close to choosing a solution to the dilemma. It is at this moment that you should introduce the 'spanner'. Read it to them and ask them to use the information provided to reconsider their decision. Give them time to deliberate properly on the new perspective that they have gained, and ensure that they integrate the ideas included into their discussions.

## Reflection on the process

The group, having made their choice, should then be given an opportunity to reflect on the process they have been through. What is important here is that students have the

chance to think through their own experience, and that of the group, properly. It is tempting to move through this element of the exercise quickly, but it is through this meta-cognitive discussion that the process of making wise choices has a real chance to develop. Therefore, students should fill in the process review sheet individually, and then come back together to discuss their work as a group. It might be useful on the first few occasions that the technique is used to list some particular areas for the students to consider on the whiteboard so that they have a clear structure to follow.

GO TO ···⫸

Find a copy of a process review sheet on p29.

## The plenary

This stage of the exercise is an opportunity for students to share their experiences. Again, it should be as student-led as possible. Each group should be given the opportunity to present both their solution, and the reasoning behind their solution. It should also be possible for the other groups to question them about their work. Possible solutions might be written up on the board, and the main ideas behind them added. The students could then be asked to vote for the solution that they think is the wisest, and could be asked to discuss this in a follow-up piece of written work.

It is crucial, however, that as well as discussing the content, the process through which the solution was arrived at is also carefully and fully considered. This meta-level discussion will make explicit the thought and group processes involved and, through the use of a reflective diary or log, the ideas can be revisited the next time the technique is used, to help develop skills further and more directly.

## Introducing the ethical element

Finally, the reflective questions included in the exercise, asking students to consider their own personal ethics, should be picked up again, and the students should be made aware of how their own beliefs are often at the core of their decision-making when encountering dilemmas. They should also be asked in follow-up work to voice and discuss these ethical frameworks so that they can begin consciously to defend and perhaps even challenge their own beliefs and assumptions about people, events, and life in general. The more we can help them reflect in these ways, the greater the chance that they might make wise, considered and reasoned decisions when they are older.

## Timings

It is vital that the students have a clear opportunity to discuss and consider both the content and the process involved in making a wise decision. For this reason students should not be made to reach conclusions quickly. An exercise such as this should be given a full two lessons (of approximately one hour each), or possibly even three, depending on the level of debate generated at each stage.

## Religious education

*This dilemma deals with the difficult decisions that people face when the life of another person is at stake. When we make such decisions, who are we making them for? Do our feelings, emotions and beliefs affect the decisions we make?*

Your partner has been rushed into hospital having suffered from emphysema for some years. They are now unable to walk and even talking is difficult. They have to remain on bottled oxygen for much of the day. Doctors are finding it hard to stablise your partner, who has already been resuscitated twice. Although your partner does seem somewhat better, they are in constant pain.

You have been told that your partner should be able to live for another four to five weeks, but that during that time they will have to be heavily sedated. Alternatively, the doctors are willing to withdraw treatment whilst keeping your partner comfortable.

They can't help you decide what to do on this occasion.

You know that your partner has made a living will asking that, if they are in severe and terminal pain, they should be allowed to die. Your children have arrived at the hospital and want your partner's treatment to continue, but do not know about the living will.

- What was your final decision?
- List the factors that made you decide as you did.
- Why did you think that these factors were important?
- If one of your children had converted to a religion that believes in the sanctity of life, how might this affect the situation? Can you understand their perspective?

Write a summary that explains your decision and the reasons behind it. Try to explain what led you to think that these reasons are so important.

*Chris Kington Publishing*

## Introducing the dilemma

Having settled the group with some form of photo-orientated odd-one-out exercise, it is time to begin the dilemma-based lesson. To begin with, the information given on p118 could be introduced on the whiteboard, and on copied sheets for the students, although the 'spanner' would not be introduced at this time. The dilemma should be read through and the students asked to spend a few minutes quietly considering the main pieces of information they have been given. Once this has been reflected upon, the students should then be invited to build a simple list or mind map on the board that highlights the key points. In this case, a consideration of the different religious views on the sanctity of life would be appropriate.

## Developing wisdom in groups

Having explicitly introduced some of the factors that might play a major part in the students' deliberation, split them up into small groups to discuss the issues and to attempt to develop a wise solution. If the exercise is being taught for the first time, or where there is little experience of the technique, the teacher might want to ask students to allocate themselves various roles to facilitate the work of the group. However, if students have used this technique before, it might be better to allow them to organise themselves. Each group is given an opportunity to use each of the Webs in turn to help scaffold their discussion. In this case study, some of the pertinent questions to highlight for students might include:

GO TO ⋯⟩

The roles are given on p7.

### The Think Web
- What makes this a dilemma?
- What are the key issues that might influence a solution?
- How many solutions can we find?

### The Me Web
- How would the main character feel?

### The Others Web
- Who else is mentioned in the dilemma?
- Is there anyone else who might be affected, but who isn't specifically mentioned?

### The Community Web
- What would happen in the long term to the local population?

This process should be used to allow the group to agree on a solution that they believe to be the wisest.

## Introducing the 'spanner'

As you walk around the room, you will begin to sense that groups are coming to some level of agreement in their work, and will be close to choosing a solution to the dilemma. It is at this moment that you should introduce the 'spanner'. Read it to them and ask them to use the information provided to reconsider their decision. Give them time to deliberate properly on the new perspective that they have gained, and ensure that they integrate the ideas included into their discussions.

GO TO ⋯⟩

For an explanation of the 'spanner' see p77.

## Reflection on the process

The group, having made their choice, should then be given an opportunity to reflect on the process they have been through. What is important here is that students have the

GO TO ⋯➤

Find a copy of a process review sheet on p29.

chance to think through their own experience, and that of the group, properly. It is tempting to move through this element of the exercise quickly, but it is through this meta-cognitive discussion that the process of making wise choices has a real chance to develop. Therefore, students should fill in the process review sheet individually, and then come back together to discuss their work as a group. It might be useful on the first few occasions that the technique is used to list some particular areas for the students to consider on the whiteboard so that they have a clear structure to follow.

## The plenary

This stage of the exercise is an opportunity for students to share their experiences. Again, it should be as student-led as possible. Each group should be given the opportunity to present both their solution, and the reasoning behind their solution. It should also be possible for the other groups to question them about their work. Possible solutions might be written up on the board, and the main ideas behind them added. The students could then be asked to vote for the solution that they think is the wisest, and could be asked to discuss this in a follow-up piece of written work.

It is crucial, however, that as well as discussing the content, the process through which the solution was arrived at is also carefully and fully considered. This meta-level discussion will make explicit the thought and group processes involved and, through the use of a reflective diary or log, the ideas can be revisited the next time the technique is used, to help develop skills further and more directly.

## Introducing the ethical element

Finally, the reflective questions included in the exercise, asking students to consider their own personal ethics, should be picked up again, and the students should be made aware of how their own beliefs are often at the core of their decision-making when encountering dilemmas. They should also be asked in follow-up work to voice and discuss these ethical frameworks so that they can begin consciously to defend and perhaps even challenge their own beliefs and assumptions about people, events, and life in general. The more we can help them reflect in these ways, the greater the chance that they might make wise, considered and reasoned decisions when they are older.

## Timings

It is vital that the students have a clear opportunity to discuss and consider both the content and the process involved in making a wise decision. For this reason students should not be made to reach conclusions quickly. An exercise such as this should be given a full two lessons (of approximately one hour each), or possibly even three, depending on the level of debate generated at each stage.

**Geography**

**Case Study 3**

*This dilemma highlights the problems facing charities every day when they have to make difficult decisions – often without all the facts in front of them. What price can be put on a single human life?*

You work for an aid agency which is attempting to provide emergency aid to a country ripped apart by civil war. The people of the country have suffered greatly, and civilians on both sides are dying in their thousands.

Because of the war, crops have not been planted to the extent required to feed everyone, and many areas of farmland have been peppered with landmines. You know that emergency aid has been flown in to the north of the country, but you are attempting to help those in the south. You now have the help of a local leader to do so.

You have the ability to offer different types of aid, such as food, medical supplies and fuel, but rumour has it that local militias on both sides are plundering much of the aid for their own use, with little getting through to the people who need it.

Your workers in the region need a quick decision.

There are rumours that the local leader who is brokering the deal with you is a rebel leader who has been involved in massacres across the country for the past three years. However, these rumours have emerged from the north of the country, governed by people who oppose his political party.

**Geography**

- What was your final decision?
- List the factors that made you decide as you did.
- Why did you think that these factors were important?
- Is it possible to take what the media say in any country as the truth?
- Can it ever be right to work with a tyrant if it means that innocent people might live?

Write a summary that explains your decision and the reasons behind it. Try to explain what led you to think that these reasons are so important.

## Introducing the dilemma

Having settled the group with some form of photo-orientated odd-one-out exercise, it is time to begin the dilemma-based lesson. To begin with, the information given on p121 could be introduced on the whiteboard, and on copied sheets for the students, although the 'spanner' would not be introduced at this time. The dilemma should be read through and the students asked to spend a few minutes quietly considering the main pieces of information they have been given. Once this has been reflected upon, the students should then be invited to build a simple list or mind map on the board that highlights the key points. In this case, it might be interesting to ask the students to list conflicts that are currently in the news, and to see if they know what forms of aid are given to those areas, if any.

## Developing wisdom in groups

Having explicitly introduced some of the factors that might play a major part in the students' deliberation, split them up into small groups to discuss the issues and to attempt to develop a wise solution. If the exercise is being taught for the first time, or where there is little experience of the technique, the teacher might want to ask students to allocate themselves various roles to facilitate the work of the group. However, if students have used this technique before, it might be better to allow them to organise themselves. Each group is given an opportunity to use each of the Webs in turn to help scaffold their discussion. In this case study, some of the pertinent questions to highlight for students might include:

GO TO ⋯⋗

The roles are given on p7.

### The Think Web

- What makes this a dilemma?
- What are the key issues that might influence a solution?
- How many solutions can we find?

### The Me Web

- How would the main character feel?

### The Others Web

- Who else is mentioned in the dilemma?
- Is there anyone else who might be affected, but who isn't specifically mentioned?

### The Community Web

- What would happen in the long term to the local population?

This process should be used to allow the group to agree on a solution that they believe to be the wisest.

## Introducing the 'spanner'

As you walk around the room, you will begin to sense that groups are coming to some level of agreement in their work, and will be close to choosing a solution to the dilemma. It is at this moment that you should introduce the 'spanner'. Read it to them and ask them to use the information provided to reconsider their decision. Give them time to deliberate properly on the new perspective that they have gained, and ensure that they integrate the ideas included into their discussions.

GO TO ⋯⋗

For an explanation of the 'spanner' see p77.

## Reflection on the process

The group, having made their choice, should then be given an opportunity to reflect on the process they have been through. What is important here is that students have the

chance to think through their own experience, and that of the group, properly. It is tempting to move through this element of the exercise quickly, but it is through this meta-cognitive discussion that the process of making wise choices has a real chance to develop. Therefore, students should fill in the process review sheet individually, and then come back together to discuss their work as a group. It might be useful on the first few occasions that the technique is used to list some particular areas for the students to consider on the whiteboard so that they have a clear structure to follow.

GO TO ···$\rightarrow$

Find a copy of a process review sheet on p29.

## The plenary

This stage of the exercise is an opportunity for students to share their experiences. Again, it should be as student-led as possible. Each group should be given the opportunity to present both their solution, and the reasoning behind their solution. It should also be possible for the other groups to question them about their work. Possible solutions might be written up on the board, and the main ideas behind them added. The students could then be asked to vote for the solution that they think is the wisest, and could be asked to discuss this in a follow-up piece of written work.

It is crucial, however, that as well as discussing the content, the process through which the solution was arrived at is also carefully and fully considered. This meta-level discussion will make explicit the thought and group processes involved and, through the use of a reflective diary or log, the ideas can be revisited the next time the technique is used, to help develop skills further and more directly.

## Introducing the ethical element

Finally, the reflective questions included in the exercise, asking students to consider their own personal ethics, should be picked up again, and the students should be made aware of how their own beliefs are often at the core of their decision-making when encountering dilemmas. They should also be asked in follow-up work to voice and discuss these ethical frameworks so that they can begin consciously to defend and perhaps even challenge their own beliefs and assumptions about people, events, and life in general. The more we can help them reflect in these ways, the greater the chance that they might make wise, considered and reasoned decisions when they are older.

## Timings

It is vital that the students have a clear opportunity to discuss and consider both the content and the process involved in making a wise decision. For this reason students should not be made to reach conclusions quickly. An exercise such as this should be given a full two lessons (of approximately one hour each), or possibly even three, depending on the level of debate generated at each stage.

*Chris Kington Publishing*

# Personalising dilemmas – taking the essence of a key dilemma and applying it to new situations

As stated in Sections 1 and 2, the best dilemmas are those developed by teachers to suit their own contexts. In this section, suggestions are made as to how you might use examples of dilemmas from news events, historical knowledge, syllabus content, etc and 'personalise' these to the life experiences of the students themselves. When working with teachers across all subject areas, we have noticed an understandable tendency to lift huge, almost literally world-shaking dilemmas from history (eg the decision to drop the atomic bomb on Hiroshima and Nagasaki), or content-tied dilemmas from a course syllabus or schemes of work (eg in Steinbeck's *Of Mice and Men*, George's advice to the impressionable Lennie, who is in hiding after committing a crime and is armed).

Enticing as this may be in curriculum terms, the risk here is that students fail to relate these scenarios to their own lives – it's not easy to empathise with an American President in 1945, nor with an armed fugitive. Moreover, the more content-specific the dilemmas selected, the less likely the students will be to see the activity as genuinely open-ended, challenging and amenable to their own creativity and intellectual effort – if there's an 'answer' in history, literature, etc, what's the point of creating alternatives? Many students would in these circumstances sooner simply 'learn' the 'correct' solution from traditional routes.

It is preferable, instead, to approach curriculum learning 'from round the back' – presenting students with a dilemma to which they can relate, and only afterwards connecting this to the content-area. This can be achieved by following (or adapting) these steps:

## 1. Surveying

Review the syllabus for dilemma-rich material (moments where difficult choices, with no clear 'right' answer have to be made, and that require the processing of complex, often conflicting data). Identify one or more possibilities for further study.

## 2. Extracting the 'essence'

Consider the dilemmas identified above, and establish the core features that define the dilemma. For example, take the decision to drop the first atomic bombs: at its heart this dilemma revolves around the concept of 'least harm' – once a country was in possession of nuclear capabilities, there was no obvious 'right' way of responding to the choice this new capability presented. Which is the 'least worst' action to take? There are only two chief choices – is it better to commit further allied soldiers' lives to certain death by pursuing the war through conventional means, or to commit Japanese civilian lives to the fatal consequences of an atomic strike? Beyond these two choices, there are infinitely nuanced variations, affecting issues of morality, ethics and personal values, as well as more clinical 'problem-solving' factors – considerations such as the relative worth of human life (what proportion of American to Japanese lives saved and lost would be considered sufficient to merit the dropping of the bomb?), tactical considerations (how long to wait for unconditional – or conditional – surrender before dropping the second – or third, or fourth – bomb?), political considerations (the involvement of other allied forces in decision-making, consequences for changed relationships with these allies – eg the Soviet Union), etc.

## 3. Relating the 'essence' to a student-focused scenario

Take the concept of 'least harm' and translate this into a scenario that speaks to the students' own lives: eg Jackie has a long-standing conflict with a peer (over money, a boyfriend, etc) that shows no sign of concluding quickly or painlessly, and which is affecting a number of her relationships. She becomes party to some information that is potentially damaging to her 'enemy's' reputation/life chances/peer relationships. Jackie will need to live with the consequences of her actions. Should she proceed to use this information, or sit on it? If she should choose to use it, how will she do so? What alternatives are there? What factors does she need to take into consideration? (cf the role here for the Webs of Meaning in deliberately complicating the decision yet further.)

[The usual dilemma-based learning procedures come into play at this point.]

## 4. Inviting connections

Ask the students, following the dilemma-based learning plenary/group feedback, to relate this experience and their decisions back to the core curricular event from which the dilemma was extracted. Get them to reflect on connections and distinctions – eg how is this dilemma similar to President Truman's and distinct from it? How might the dilemma be improved for future use? An adapted version of Edward de Bono's PMI thinking tool might be helpful in this regard:

| **Connections** (ways in which it is similar) | **Distinctions** (ways in which it is different) | **To Consider** (suggestions for possible improvement) |
|---|---|---|
| | | |
| | | |
| | | |
| | | |
| | | |
| | | |
| | | |
| | | |
| | | |

As a valuable extension or homework activity, steps 1-3 above can be set for the students to do themselves. It is a demanding task, requiring high-level thinking, from the concrete to the abstract and back to the concrete. In terms of potential learning gains (both curriculum-focused and metacognitive), however, its value is inestimable. It saves you a bit of time too!

*Chris Kington Publishing*

# Beyond dilemmas – applying learning to thinking and life

## Getting students to think

It is important that dilemma-based learning is seen first and foremost as a framework for thinking. The dilemmas themselves are the context for a profound form of thought. It is important not to rush the exercises as the action of debate and thought is essentially what is being developed and considered here.

This should also be seen as a starting point for students to be more thoughtful beyond the classroom. In debriefing them once an exercise has finished, emphasis should be on discussion of the process of thinking and decision-making and how this should lead them to consider issues in a more reflective way. As such, we are not advocating a specific skill, such as critical thinking, etc, but a more general ability to use thought to consider and make wiser decisions whenever required.

## Situations for developing wisdom

To get students thinking, we can use many and varied situations to help them, not only in a humanities classroom. It is often the case, even in a short morning registration period, that students are constantly grappling with dilemmas, and often the distressed mood in which we find students comes from a lack of thought or ability to deal with those dilemmas.

Therefore, the situations we can discuss and debate with students that help to develop their wisdom are almost countless. While the 'staged' dilemmas that constitute the focus of this book are excellent in making learning more relevant and in helping students to learn those thought processes that will aid them beyond school, there is no reason why events in the lives of students shouldn't allow for an impromptu debate and a reflection on positive ways of considering the dilemmas in which they find themselves.

## Getting students to understand the generic nature of the exercises and the skills/competences they develop

The debrief of any dilemma-based learning exercise is perhaps one of the most important parts of the experience. It is here that students can be helped to understand the generic issues and ideas that form the basis to much of what we have discussed here. All children need both support and guidance to make sense of their world, and this technique is no different. It helps to provide a structure for them to make good choices in their lives. But this is very much an end-point, and it is through consistent and prolonged discussion and the opportunity to try out the dawning skills and understanding that are so important. Perhaps some of the most important elements that students can learn include:

- a greater understanding of the complexity of life
- an understanding that not all choices are about good or bad, but might be about good versus better, or even bad versus worse
- a framework of questions that might help in making decisions in complex situations
- the ability to reflect and contemplate before making decisions
- an understanding that often a decision is not the only correct answer and that others who take a different path may be equally justified in doing so
- an understanding that working with others on a problem or issue may actually result in a greater degree of clarity for the individual
- an understanding that our ethical outlook on life influences our perspectives on dilemmas and issues, and that we therefore need constantly to address our own prejudices and assumptions.

## How can this help in our day-to-day lives?

Children are often naive about the workings of the world about them, often taking on trust what they are told – by parents, by the media, by adults in general. They are also located in an increasingly complex world, where being reflective and wise are not necessarily traits that are highly prized. However, this is the time that a capacity to step back from situations, think things through and make wise decisions, looking forward a month or a year, becomes important. The techniques covered and exemplified in this book are concerned with helping develop confident, critically minded individuals who can work cooperatively with others, and see the benefit in doing so. It is in this sense that dilemma-based learning can contribute towards this end.

# Dilemma-based learning beyond the classroom – using Webs of Meaning for complex decision-making

The potential of the dilemma-based learning approach for decision-making would be underused if it was only an occasionally used approach within one or two subject departments. The importance of ensuring a balanced approach to decision-making within schools can not be underestimated, as schools are complex organisations with many conflicting interests. The Webs of Meaning provide a structure for decision-making that can be used where group decision-making is required. This might include using the Webs of Meaning structure when complex decisions need to be made in:

- class and school councils
- student decision-making in clubs and societies
- school leadership teams
- subject department meetings.

A structure for using dilemma-based learning for real-life decision-making might involve the following steps:

1. Identify the time that will be available for discussions and allocate time for exploring the issue within each Web.
2. Agree roles – one member of the group should act as Web master. It will be their role to:
   - keep time and change the Web when appropriate
   - encourage participants to keep to the 'spirit' of the Web so that enquiry is focused on the Web categories (Think, Others, Me, Community and Balance).
3. The Webs should be kept in a pile on the table and turned over in turn. Participants should start with the Think Web to identify as many options as possible and agree a limited number for further investigation – within all of the Webs.
4. The Balance Web should be used to allow participants to formulate the wisest solution.

## The dilemma-based learning approach to improving behaviour

The dilemma-based learning approach can be used to support students who exhibit challenging behaviour. This approach is based upon the idea that most incidents of challenging behaviour can be reframed as students making unwise choices about their behaviour. Each school will identify its own approach but this might include the following elements:

- Small-group work for students involved in incidents of poor behaviour – this provides an opportunity for students to reflect upon real-life incidents of poor behaviour and use dilemma-based learning to identify more appropriate responses. The first task would be to reframe the incident by identifying the dilemma/choice that was being made.

- Following incidents of challenging behaviour, students should be asked to reflect with an adult (or Web facilitator) upon the incident using the Webs of Meaning. For example, following an incident where a student swore at a member of staff, the student would be encouraged to complete the following process:
  - The first task is for the student to describe the incident in detail in a chronological sequence and decide upon a decision point where the student's choice led to the poor behaviour. Exploration using dilemma-based learning should centre around this choice.

- Webs of Meaning cards (see photocopiable resource, p167-173) should be placed on a table in front of the student who should turn over them in sequence starting with the Think Web. This provides an opportunity for identifying as many options as possible and choosing two or three for further investigation. This should include the choice made by the student that led to the poor behaviour.

- As the cards are turned over, the options are explored from the perspective of each of the Webs of Meaning.

- Finally, when the Balance Web is turned, the student and facilitator decide on the wisest choice possible.

The example on p131 shows how a post-incident debrief session might be structured using the Webs of Meaning. It is important that the session is only embarked upon when emotions have calmed. In most cases, this will be the following day.

The process might be used in a small-group situation, through a 'Friendship Web'. This would be a selected group of students who support each other in making wise choices about work and behaviour. These groups can take part in a range of team-building activities, as well as exploring real-life scenario exploration with the Webs of Meaning.

Dilemma-based learning provides a structured and practical way of supporting decision-making processes across the school, whether it is the individual making a choice about their behaviour or more strategic decision-making in school councils or staff meetings. This section provides some ideas but recognises that there are many uses for the Webs of Meaning. We believe that the natural creativity of those in schools will develop and extend their use.

# Example of a post-incident debrief session using the Webs of Meaning

## The incident

On Monday, period 8, Kerry was in science. She started to disrupt the lesson. Initially, this involved chatting with peers but when they started work she became more disruptive. She stole another student's book and hid it. When the teacher challenged Kerry, she argued back and said it wasn't her fault and the teacher was always picking on her. The teacher eventually gave her a choice, to settle to work or face detention. Five minutes later, Kerry was giggling with a friend. When the teacher gave her a detention slip, Kerry jumped up and swore, before running from the room, kicking over a chair as she went.

## Dilemma (from Kerry's perspective)

I wanted to work but couldn't because I had missed the last two lessons. Everyone else was working and when I asked for help from my best friend she told me to shut up. My dilemma was that I wanted to work but I couldn't.

## Think Web (identifying Kerry's options)

1. Keep going on at my friend and when she doesn't respond, steal her book. Then she will have to help me.

2. Sit quietly and pretend to be getting on.

3. Explain to the teacher what had happened.

4. Ask another person in the class for help.

## Think Web (exploration)

### Me Web

### Others Web (teacher, friend, other children)

### Community Web

Each Web will be used to explore the three favoured options. Make sure that the option that led to the challenging behaviour is included.

## Balance Web

The student and facilitator state their favoured option.

# Reflecting and planning for dilemma-based learning

This section is intended to support those individuals who have tried some of the more advanced ideas in their classrooms and beyond, and who want to reflect on their successes and areas for development.

## Initial reflections

If you have tried some of the issues in this section, consider:

- Who did you try the approach with?
- How successful was it?
- How difficult was it to introduce the idea of ethics to students?
- What do you feel they have gained from a discussion of ethics?
- How did you incorporate ideas about ethics into your students' work?
- How well were students able to reflect on their ethical beliefs?
- Where this didn't work very well, can you suggest why not? Where it worked well, why was this so?
- Would you do anything differently next time?
- If you have tried to use dilemma-based learning in a more practical context, how did the students react to it?

## Planning for the future

In planning for the future, perhaps consider:

- What elements of dilemma-based learning have you and the students enjoyed?
- Are there any other situations in which you might want to use dilemma-based learning?
- What elements of your programme of study or examination best relate to the aims and methods of the technique?

| Table of example ethical dilemmas | | |
|---|---|---|
| **Examples of ethical history dilemmas** | | |
| Example 1 | The execution of Louis XVI | 133 |
| Example 2 | Black people in America | 135 |
| Example 3 | Women's suffrage | 137 |
| Example 4 | The Stalinist Purges | 139 |
| **Examples of ethical religious education dilemmas** | | |
| Example 1 | A utilitarian dilemma | 141 |
| Example 2 | Animal rights | 143 |
| Example 3 | Euthanasia | 145 |
| Example 4 | Free speech | 147 |
| **Examples of ethical geography dilemmas** | | |
| Example 1 | Reacting to hazards | 149 |
| Example 2 | Economic rise of China | 151 |
| Example 3 | Agriculture | 153 |
| Example 4 | Global warming | 155 |

*Chris Kington Publishing*

# Examples of ethical history dilemmas

## The execution of Louis XVI — Example 1

As a member of a Convention court, you have been asked to vote on whether or not to execute your king. The king has already been found guilty of several charges. These include bankrupting your country, being disloyal to a new constitution (created when your country was declared a republic) and of plotting against the Revolution – of which you are a part. Not only this, but he has been caught trying to escape the country with his family, and is suspected of supporting another country's army against you. However, he is still your king, anointed by God.

How do you vote?

There are rumours that bad decisions taken by the National Assembly have been blamed on the king. Is it a good idea to be seen to support him?

Consider the following:

- What was your final decision?

- List the factors that made you decide as you did.

- Why did you think that these factors were the most important?

- Is it ever right to execute a human being for political ends?

- Should we stand up for what we believe to be true, even if this puts us in danger?

Write a summary explaining your decision and the reasons behind it. Try to include the beliefs you have from reflecting on the questions above and incorporate this into your reasoning.

## The execution of Louis XVI — Example 1

###  Background

This dilemma gets students to question constitutional law and the kind of dilemmas that were involved in shaping revolutionary France. It also highlights the need for individuals to be seen to make the 'correct' choice. Can we condemn them for acting unethically?

###  Context

This dilemma could introduce the study of Louis XVI and his part in the French Revolution. It has been deliberately 'anonymised' so that the general issues can be considered before going on to study the detail of the historical events.

###  Focus

This exercise asks students to consider whether ethical choices are sometimes overridden by pragmatism.

###  Webs

All of the Webs would be useful in this exercise. However, if this is to be a brief exercise, particular focus could be given to the:
- Others Web
- Think Web
- Community Web

###  Questions

This exercise engages students in personal reflection once they have completed the exercise. They may want to consider:
- Why did I/we make the decision I/we did?
- Did I change my point of view once I had all the facts?

###  Following up

Follow-up work could develop in many directions. Two possible directions are:
- Ask students to research the events leading up to the trial of Louis XVI.
- Ask students to consider which of these events played a major role in his eventual execution.

## Black people in America

**Example 2**

You are head of a company transporting cargo from Africa to America. It is a very profitable trade, which has helped to pay for your lovely nine-bedroom house and a new office at the port. However, you tend to lose part of the cargo on most journeys.

Do you go to much greater expense to save a small portion of your load?

It is 1758 and your 'cargo' consists of African slaves who are being sent to the West Indies.

Consider the following:

- What was your final decision?

- List the factors that made you decide as you did.

- Why did you think that these factors were the most important?

- What is slavery, and is it still happening today?

- Why do most people find slavery ethically repugnant?

Write a summary explaining your decision and the reasons behind it. Try to include the beliefs you have from reflecting on the questions above and incorporate this into your reasoning.

## Black people in America

Example 2

 **Background**

This dilemma outlines the way in which slave traders saw slaves as a commodity rather than as human beings.

 **Context**

This dilemma could introduce the slave trade and its treatment of the slaves if transported.

 **Focus**

This exercise is focused on the 'spanner', used to set up a clear instance of cognitive conflict in the students, as they realise that their discussion of a 'commodity' is actually about people. This then leads to a wider ranging ethical consideration of slavery in general.

 **Webs**

All of the Webs would be useful in this exercise. However, if this is to be a brief exercise, particular focus could be given to the:
• Me Web
• Others Web
• Community Web

 **Questions**

This exercise engages students in personal reflection once they have completed the exercise. They may want to consider:
• What factors did I/we find most important in making my/our initial decision?
• How did the 'spanner' change my/our view of the dilemma?

 **Following up**

Follow-up work could develop in many directions. Two possible directions are:
• Ask students to research how the slaves taken from Africa were treated and the resultant hardship, death, etc this caused. Also consider how traders attempted to rationalise this.
• Ask students to research an example of 'modern slavery'. How does it compare to what happened in the 16th and 17th centuries, and are the excuses used still the same?

## Women's suffrage

Example 3

You come into school one warm summer's morning. You make your way, as normal, to your tutor room, and when you arrive your teacher is there to meet you at the door. As you come into the room your teacher tells you that you are to vote for a year representative on the student council. However, only half of you can vote as the school feels that it would be better to restrict the number of voters.

The teacher asks how you would like to decide which students are to vote – and for future reference, whether you feel this is a fair system or not.

A late note arrives with another student. It appears that all other tutor groups in the school have decided that only boys can vote. Will you accept this?

Consider the following:

- What was your final decision?

- List the factors that made you decide as you did.

- Why did you think that these factors were the most important?

- Is it ever right to exclude one sex from activities open to the other?

- Is it ethically right that we see males and females as equal?

Write a summary explaining your decision and the reasons behind it. Try to include the beliefs you have from reflecting on the questions above and incorporate this into your reasoning.

## Women's suffrage

Example 3

###  Background

This dilemma focuses on the inequalities that led to the women's suffrage movement. What were the arguments made by both sides for protecting or dismantling unfair social and political structures?

###  Context

This dilemma acts as an introduction to the issue of women's suffrage, by putting students in the position of deciding on issues of equality.

###  Focus

This exercise considers equality and the reasons behind universal suffrage. By leaving the gender element until the 'spanner' is introduced, students may well find ways of rationalising the choices they need to make, but no doubt the gender element will lead to renewed arguments, which will rehearse many of the arguments, used in the early 20th century.

###  Webs

All of the Webs would be useful in this exercise. However, if this is to be a brief exercise, particular focus could be given to the:
- Me Web
- Others Web
- Think Web

###  Questions

This exercise engages students in personal reflection once they have completed the exercise. They may want to consider:
- What factors did I/we find most important in making my/our initial decision?
- Why are some forms of division more repellent to us than others?

###  Following up

Follow-up work could develop in many directions. Two possible directions are:
- Ask students to research the reasons given by the women's suffrage movement for universal suffrage, and the counter-arguments offered by some politicians.
- Ask students to consider the extent to which inequalities still exist in politics and society. Who are some of the modern-day campaigners against such inequality?

## The Stalinist Purges

**Example 4**

You are a member of a committee at school, responsible for working with the staff on issues of behaviour and sanctions. You chair the committee, and have the power to select other members once every month.

At one meeting, you bring forward a new idea to allow students to chew gum in lessons. Four of the committee members say that they don't agree with you and vote against it, stopping the idea from going forward to the staff.

This makes you angry. You have the power to get rid of them for the next meeting, when you can have the vote again.

What do you do?

---

The secretary of the committee talks to you quietly after and says that you should think very carefully about what you do. The secretary can be asked to leave as well if you wish!

---

Consider the following:

- What was your final decision?

- List the factors that made you decide as you did.

- Why did you think that these factors were the most important?

- Is it right for a single person to have ultimate power over others?

- What might be the consequences of such power?

Write a summary explaining your decision and the reasons behind it. Try to include the beliefs you have from reflecting on the questions above and incorporate this into your reasoning.

## The Stalinist Purges

Example 4

###  Background

This dilemma considers the reasons for Stalin's Purges by thinking about the obvious advantages that absolute power can bring, especially by removing anyone who might challenge the policies of the leader.

###  Context

This dilemma introduces Stalin's Purges by using a format that can be seen as simple but analogous to the Purges themselves, acting as a bridge to a more formal consideration of the period.

###  Focus

This exercise asks students to consider the effects that having too much power might have in terms of decision-making and, once a course has been set, how easy it becomes to continue to make such decisions. It also asks students to consider whether they think it is ever right to have absolute power over others.

###  Webs

All of the Webs would be useful in this exercise. However, if this is to be a brief exercise, particular focus could be given to the:
• Me Web
• Others Web
• Balance Web

###  Questions

This exercise engages students in personal reflection once they have completed the exercise. They may want to consider:
• What factors did I/we find most important in making my/our initial decision?
• Was there discussion about the level of power that the chairperson of the committee had?

###  Following up

Follow-up work could develop in many directions. Two possible directions are:
• Ask students to research Stalin's Purges. How could they have happened, and what were the consequences?
• Ask students to consider if it is ever possible for a despot, or ruler with absolute power, to be benevolent?

# Examples of ethical religious education dilemmas

**A utilitarian dilemma**

**Example 1**

You are a paramedic driving home late at night at the end of a shift. Coming round a bend in the road, you see two cars in front of you that have obviously been involved in a crash. There is smoke coming from the crash site, but there is no fire.

As you approach, you see that in one car there is an old woman, unconscious and obviously very badly hurt. In the other, there is a young man, also unconscious. You recognise him – he's a very well-known film star. It is obvious that you can only help one of them survive, but who?

As you get really close to the cars, you recognise the woman. She works at the local hospital and is a world-famous heart surgeon.

Consider the following:

- What was your final decision?

- List the factors that made you decide as you did.

- Why did you think that these factors were the most important?

- To what extent was your choice made in relation to the amount of happiness and worth these people would bring to others?

- Is there a better way than this to make such a decision?

Write a summary explaining your decision and the reasons behind it. Try to include the beliefs you have from reflecting on the questions above and incorporate this into your reasoning.

## A utilitarian dilemma  Example 1

 **Background**

This dilemma outlines a classic utilitarian problem. Who should the paramedic save? Both individuals bring happiness to others – but in very different ways. Added to this is the conflict caused by the 'spanner', which makes the decision far more difficult, and can also be used to consider Mill's 'higher' and 'lower' order of happiness, the higher order happiness being intellectual, the lower being more 'base'.

**Context**

This dilemma introduces utilitarianism and the primacy of happiness as a model for ethical behaviour.

 **Focus**

This exercise focuses on the disadvantages of making an ethical decision when using utilitarianism as the basis for 'calculation'.

 **Webs**

All of the Webs would be useful in this exercise. However, if this is to be a brief exercise, particular focus could be given to the:
• Me Web
• Others Web
• Community Web

 **Questions**

This exercise engages students in personal reflection once they have completed the exercise. They may want to consider:
• What factors did I/we find most important in making my/our initial decision?
• Am I/we satisfied with my/our decision?
• Is this possible in this case?

 **Following up**

Follow-up work could develop in many directions. Two possible directions are:
• Ask students to investigate in more detail the different approaches possible in utilitarian ethics and how they might affect their final decision.
• Ask students to consider the extent to which they feel utilitarianism provides a useful ethical decision-making framework.

## Animal rights

**Example 2**

You have just played sport for your school team and have been invited round to a friend's house for a meal. You haven't had time to get cleaned up because the game went on so long, so your friend's parents have said that you can have a shower at their home.

When you arrive, you go up to the bathroom, and have a quick shower, using some shampoo that your parents have put in your bag. When you have finished, you get dressed and go down stairs, forgetting to put the shampoo away. Your friend's older sister sees the shampoo and later tells you that it is tested on animals. She asks you if you will stop using it and use a different brand in future.

How do you respond?

_____

You are having this conversation at the dinner table. You notice that your friend's sister is eating a nice piece of beef.

_____

Consider the following:

- What was your final decision?

- List the factors that made you decide as you did.

- Why did you think that these factors were the most important?

- To what extent was your choice informed by your views on the intelligence and rights of the animals involved?

- Is there a difference between animal testing and the use of animals for food? If so why?

Write a summary explaining your decision and the reasons behind it. Try to include the beliefs you have from reflecting on the questions above and incorporate this into your reasoning.

## Animal rights

**Example 2**

###  Background

This dilemma outlines the issue of animal rights. At what point should animal rights be seen as legitimate? This has been made more immediate by locating the dilemma in a scenario that could be directly experienced by students.

###  Context

This dilemma introduces the issue of animal rights. It can help students to think about the spectrum of rights that different groups feel are legitimate, such as those against cosmetics testing, or those people who are vegetarian. It can then act as a basis for considering how this issue relates to religious beliefs.

###  Focus

This exercise asks students to consider and reflect on the extent to which they believe animals should have rights. Is it OK to experiment on animals if it is for drugs development, cosmetics or for food?

###  Webs

All of the Webs would be useful in this exercise. However, if this is to be a brief exercise, particular focus could be given to the:

- Me Web
- Others Web
- Think Web

###  Questions

This exercise engages students in personal reflection once they have completed the exercise. They may want to consider:

- What factors did I/we find most important in making my/our initial decision?
- What level of rights do I/we believe animals should have and why?

###  Following up

Follow-up work could develop in many directions. Two possible directions are:

- Ask students to research the beliefs of the main religions, with regard to animal rights.
- Ask students to consider their own ethical beliefs concerning animal rights and why they hold them.

*Chris Kington Publishing*

## Euthanasia

**Example 3**

You make your way to the private room as you do every day. Your aunt is sitting up in bed, her arm attached to the drip. She looks a little better today, but still a number of machines monitor her condition. She is obviously in a great deal of pain. One of her doctors tells you that she is terminally ill and only has a couple of months to live. She is in a great deal of pain – even the drugs in the drip do not help her to remain comfortable. On returning to her room, you find that she has slipped into unconsciousness. The doctor says that it is doubtful whether she will regain consciousness. The law of your country allows for a family member to give consent for doctors to terminate a patient's life.

What do you do?

Your aunt is a very religious person, who believes in the sanctity of life.

Consider the following:

- What was your final decision?

- List the factors that made you decide as you did.

- Why did you think that these factors were the most important?

- Do you think it is ever right to take another person's life?

- What rules should govern euthanasia and why?

Write a summary explaining your decision and the reasons behind it. Try to include the beliefs you have from reflecting on the questions above and incorporate this into your reasoning.

## Euthanasia

Example 3

###  Background

This dilemma focuses on the issue of euthanasia by asking students to assume the part of a family member. Students then explore their views about assisted death.

###  Context

This dilemma introduces the ethics of euthanasia, acting as a basis for an enquiry into the beliefs of the main world religions.

###  Focus

This exercise shows the difficulties involved in making choices in a situation where no simple conclusion can be reached. The 'spanner' also forces the students to consider the wishes of others who may have a very different ethical compass to themselves.

###  Webs

All of the Webs would be useful in this exercise. However, if this is to be a brief exercise, particular focus could be given to the:
- Me Web
- Others Web
- Balance Web

###  Questions

This exercise engages students in personal reflection once they have completed the exercise. They may want to consider:
- What factors did I/we find most important in making my/our initial decision?
- How did my/our decision change, if at all, when the 'spanner' was introduced?
- Why did you respond in the way you did?

###  Following up

Follow-up work could develop in many directions. Two possible directions are:
- Ask students to research the beliefs of the main world religions with regards to euthanasia. What arguments are put forward to support their beliefs?
- Ask students to consider their own ethical beliefs concerning the use of euthanasia in medicine?

*Chris Kington Publishing*

## Free speech

Example 4

As you come out of your place of worship, on your holy day, you notice an individual across the road loudly proclaiming that they disagree with your religious beliefs. They seem to have collected a small crowd who quietly listen.

You don't recognise them, and they are not dressed in any distinctive way. Their rant does not proclaim a certain religion or religious belief to be better than yours, but they are forceful in their condemnation of your beliefs.

What do you do?

They begin to make very inaccurate comments about your religion's beliefs. You also notice that there is a discreet police presence, obviously monitoring the situation.

Consider the following:

• What was your final decision?

• List the factors that made you decide as you did.

• Why did you think that these factors were the most important?

• To what extent should any individual have the right of free speech?

• In your opinion, at what point is the boundary of free speech crossed? Is this a boundary that should exist for all, regardless of their particular beliefs or religion?

Write a summary explaining your decision and the reasons behind it. Try to include the beliefs you have from reflecting on the questions above and incorporate this into your reasoning.

## Free speech

Example 4

###  Background

This dilemma outlines the issues that surround the criticism and discussion of religious beliefs. Should all belief systems be given the same rights and protections? In some countries this right is enshrined in law (eg USA). In others, there are complex laws concerning the content and intent of speeches (eg UK).

###  Context

This dilemma considers the extent to which free speech needs to be balanced against issues of blasphemy and people's beliefs.

###  Focus

This exercise asks students to consider the extent to which people should have the right of free speech. Is it the cornerstone of an advanced and liberal society, or should there be limits to which all people should adhere?

###  Webs

All of the Webs would be useful in this exercise. However, if this is to be a brief exercise, particular focus could be given to the:
- Me Web
- Others Web
- Community Web

###  Questions

This exercise engages students in personal reflection once they have completed the exercise. They may want to consider:
- What factors did I/we find most important in making my/our initial decision?
- Is free speech a crucial element of a modern, tolerant society or should it be managed?

###  Following up

Follow-up work could develop in many directions. Two possible directions are:
- Ask students to research the reaction of religious and cultural groups to the issue of free speech, using current affairs as a starting point.
- Ask students to consider the extent to which they believe free speech should be enshrined in law.

# Examples of ethical geography dilemmas

**Reacting to hazards**                                    **Example 1**

You are the regional director of planning for a country in south-east Asia, located on the edge of the Pacific. Within your region is a small volcanic island on which 400 people live. They make their living through a combination of fishing, farming and small-scale mineral exploitation, located on the flanks of the volcano.

However, the volcano is active, and when it erupts it does so violently. The local population wants to remain on the island, but during the last three eruptions a number of islanders were killed and the remaining population had to be evacuated – at great expense.

If the islanders were forced to leave, they would need to be resettled in the regional capital.

What would you advise the regional government to do?

_____

Local seismologists inform you that a large eruption is forecast in the next six months, but the islanders are gaining a great deal of media support to stay on the island.

_____

Consider the following:

• What was your final decision?

• List the factors that made you decide as you did.

• Why did you think that these factors were the most important?

• To what extent should communities have the right to decide their own futures?

• In your opinion, what is the most ethical course of action for both the regional government and the islanders?

Write a summary explaining your decision and the reasons behind it. Try to include the beliefs you have from reflecting on the questions above and incorporate this into your reasoning.

## Reacting to hazards

**Example 1**

###  Background

This dilemma considers the problems that planners face when local populations in danger are not keen on leaving their homes. It also explores the dilemma faced by those populations who are willing to live with a hazard to gain a good standard of living, one they would lose if they had to leave for another location.

###  Context

This dilemma considers the human impacts of hazards, particularly the dilemmas faced by planners and politicians when trying to protect populations.

###  Focus

This exercise is focused on the complexities involved in making a decision that suits everyone. Also, both parties have big ethical issues to face: should planners have and use the right to 'evict' people from their homes? Should the islanders use scarce financial resources to help themselves, when that money could be used elsewhere?

###  Webs

All of the Webs would be useful in this exercise. However, if this is to be a brief exercise, particular focus could be given to the:
- Think Web
- Balance Web
- Community Web

###  Questions

This exercise engages students in personal reflection once they have completed the exercise. They may want to consider:
- What factors did I/we find most important in making my/our initial decision?
- If the islanders want to stay, do I/we have a duty to help them if they have been made aware of the risks involved?

###  Following up

Follow-up work could develop in many directions. Two possible directions are:
- Ask students to research a hazard-planning case study. What are the issues relating to the extent and problems of protecting populations?
- Ask students to consider the extent to which they believe governments should be responsible for protecting people from hazards?

## Economic rise of China

**Example 2**

You run a company that is keen to export its goods to China. China experienced annual economic growth of between 8% and 9% at the end of the 20th century. China's international trade rose from $122 billion in 1989 to $474 billion in 2000.

Although coastal regions (eg Guangdong) are fully integrated into the global economy, much of the interior is not. Over 800,000 of the population of the country were estimated to be earning less than $77 per year by 2003.

With such an expanding economy, your company would like to be involved in the boom, as many of your competitors are already making plans to expand into the lucrative Chinese market.

However, there have also been reports of sweatshop conditions, the suppression of unions and environmental degradation. Many of your competitors have moved to China because of the cheap cost of labour and relaxed environmental laws.

What do you advise your company to do?

_____

Your company produces solar panels and wind turbines, together with technical advice on developing renewable and sustainable housing developments.

_____

Consider the following:

- What was your final decision?

- List the factors that made you decide as you did.

- Why did you think that these factors were the most important?

- To what extent should economic decisions be affected by ethical and political factors?

- In your opinion, are there issues in helping an economy to become more sustainable, even if it has a poor human rights record?

Write a summary explaining your decision and the reasons behind it. Try to include the beliefs you have from reflecting on the questions above and incorporate this into your reasoning.

## Economic rise of China

Example 2

 **Background**

This dilemma looks at the rise of the Chinese economy. Economic growth has been rapid, but this has come at a heavy price for some. There are potential issues regarding environmental problems and human rights issues.

 **Context**

This dilemma considers development of the Chinese economy through globalisation. It focuses on the ethics of economic investment and the complex decisions that companies need to make when moving into new markets.

 **Focus**

This exercise asks students to consider the ethics facing companies when they move into a new market such as China. Should decisions purely be based on economics? Is it necessary for companies to consider the political and socio-economic issues apparent within a country? The 'spanner' then adds to this by suggesting that by entering such a market it might be possible to effect positive change.

 **Webs**

All of the Webs would be useful in this exercise. However, if this is to be a brief exercise, particular focus could be given to the:

• Think Web
• Balance Web
• Community Web

 **Questions**

This exercise engages students in personal reflection once they have completed the exercise. They may want to consider:

• What factors did I/we find most important in making my/our initial decision?
• How difficult was it for you to come to a final decision? Why?

 **Following up**

Follow-up work could develop in many directions. Two possible directions are:

• Ask students to research the rise of the Chinese economy and the factors responsible for this.
• Ask students to consider the extent to which globalisation is a positive or negative force for people in other countries, especially Less Economically Developed Countries.

**Agriculture**                                                    **Example 3**

You are visited by a grain company representative at your farm. For a number of years the company has been selling you the top-up seed you need for your land, and has been understanding on those occasions when you have had cash-flow problems.

Their representative tells you about a super-grain. It has been tested in another country and the results have been spectacular. Yields have been much larger, and the quality of the produce has led to higher prices. They admit that more fertiliser needs to be used, but much of that can be organic, if needed. There is also no proven detrimental effect on the environment. However, the seed does need to be bought every year, as it is infertile when harvested, but this shouldn't be a problem with the bigger yields.

The company knows that you have struggled to make a living these past few years but think that this could be the answer to your dreams.

What do you think?

_____

You are a smallholder in an African country. Your family are just managing to hold on to their land.

_____

Consider the following:

• What was your final decision?

• List the factors that made you decide as you did.

• Why did you think that these factors were the most important?

• Can we expect other countries to supply us with genetically modified foods when we often don't want to grow them ourselves?

• Should we be willing to buy food that doesn't look 'perfect' but is still perfectly good to eat?

Write a summary explaining your decision and the reasons behind it. Try to include the beliefs you have from reflecting on the questions above and incorporate this into your reasoning.

Example 3

###  Background

This dilemma helps students to understand the dilemmas facing farmers, especially in Less Economically Developed Countries (LEDCs), including the temptation to gain higher yields against the higher costs of using GM seeds.

###  Context

This dilemma would act as a useful exercise on the Green Revolution and GM crops.

###  Focus

This exercise considers the problems of introducing new crop types to poor areas. It is also intended to highlight our own ethics. The students will assume that they are considering an example based in a More Economically Developed Country (MEDC) until they are given the 'spanner'. Does this change their perspective? In turn, does this tell us something about the acceptance of GM crops, as long as they are grown somewhere other than where we live?

###  Webs

All of the Webs would be useful in this exercise. However, if this is to be a brief exercise, particular focus could be given to the:
- Me Web
- Others Web
- Balance Web

### Q Questions

This exercise engages students in personal reflection once they have completed the exercise. They may want to consider:
- What factors did I/we find most important in making my/our initial decision?
- Did I change my point of view once I had all the facts?

###  Following up

Follow-up work could develop in many directions. Two possible directions are:
- Ask students to research the arguments for and against GM crops in both MEDCs and LEDCs?
- Ask students to consider the potential need for GM crops, with respect to climate change.

## Global warming

**Example 4**

The government agrees that we need to reduce the amount of fossil fuel burning if we are to combat global warming. Britain is well placed to utilise wind power, which is a clean, safe and renewable source of energy. It is also cost-effective when done on a large scale.

Your local authority is proposing to build the largest wind farm in England on a hilltop four miles away from your village.

Do you sign a petition against the wind farm put together by a local action group?

---

If the proposal for the wind farm fails, the government has already earmarked a site nearby on the coast for a nuclear power plant. The village will be downwind from the plant.

---

Consider the following:

- What was your final decision?

- List the factors that made you decide as you did.

- Why did you think that these factors were the most important?

- Can we always expect other communities to take the brunt of any tough environmental decisions?

- Does everyone have a moral duty to offset the effects of global warming?

Write a summary explaining your decision and the reasons behind it. Try to include the beliefs you have from reflecting on the questions above and incorporate this into your reasoning.

## Global warming

## Example 4

###  Background

This dilemma outlines issues that are likely to affect populations with the onset of global warming. As governments look at more sustainable forms of energy, do local communities have the right to expect others to face change, or should everyone have a duty to share the costs – whatever they might be?

###  Context

This dilemma considers the energy decisions we might need to make to offset the effects of global warming.

###  Focus

This exercise demonstrates the tendency of people to want solutions to their problems only as long as these solutions don't create difficulties for them. The dilemma is one of deciding which is the lesser of two negative developments.

###  Webs

All of the Webs would be useful in this exercise. However, if this is to be a brief exercise, particular focus could be given to the:
- Think Web
- Me Web
- Community Web

###  Questions

This exercise engages students in personal reflection once they have completed the exercise. They may want to consider:
- What factors did I/we find most important in making my/our initial decision?
- Did I change my point of view once I had all the facts?

###  Following up

Follow-up work could develop in many directions. Two possible directions are:
- Ask students to research the changing energy patterns that might be required to offset global warming.
- Ask students to consider the extent to which everyone should be responsible for reducing global warming.

Chris Kington Publishing

# Theoretical and practical origins

# Theoretical and practical origins

*Reflective attention always involves judging, reasoning, deliberation; it means that the child has a question of his own and is actively engaged in seeking and selecting relevant material with which to answer it... it is discipline, or gain in power of control; that is, a habit of considering problems.*

(John Dewey)

*I use not only all the brains I have, but all that I can borrow.*

(Woodrow Wilson)

## Origins – a critical education

Dr Gilbert Burgh of Queensland University observed that:

> *To truly enter into dialogue requires that before making judgments we explore alternatives, understand different perspectives, do not accept authority without question (government pronouncements, news broadcasts, etc.) – all the things we hope that students will also value.*
>
> (Burgh, 2003)

If we accept that we really do value these things (and this is by no means assured, despite this value being the raison d'être for the Webs of Meaning approach), *why* do we value them? We argue that our formal education system seems to value, in the main, other things – curriculum coverage and measurement perhaps, and standardisation and accountabilities. These imperatives can be traced back to a dominant behaviourist psychological tradition in education, which can be seen to represent an instrumentalist, expedient orientation towards the needs of educational administrators and political systems (cf the contribution of Thorndike in the early 20th century, and critiques of current practice – eg Gould, 1984; Holzman, 1997; Dadds, 2001). We also believe, however, that many teachers and education professionals still value the less easily measurable things *because they seem important to us* – as people, as professionals and as responsible citizens in a democracy – because we know that life isn't simple, or linear, or uncontaminated by doubt or ambiguity. Our novelists often know this too:

> *The open-endedness of much of [Margaret Atwood's] fiction is also a quietly political gesture: she emphasises moments when people have a choice, and having sketched out the factors involved in such choices, and what might be at stake, she suspends the moment of decision.*
>
> (Potts, 2003)

Suspension and enquiry before judgement aren't quick or easy, but they're what make some judgements intelligent, and some unintelligent.

Between 2001 and 2003, as part of our work within the Barrow-in-Furness Education Action Zone, two of the authors (Deborah Michel and Barry Hymer) held a series of small-group enquiries with a broad range of people. These enquiries, which formed part of the BarroWise Project, sought to address a fundamental question:

> What skills, abilities and dispositions does a person need in order to be wise within our local community?

We examined this question collaboratively. We worked in groups composed of older and younger children, with groups of teachers, teaching assistants and parents, and with elderly members of the local community. We explored practical dilemmas, created within the PSHE field. Some of our richest enquiries involved cross-generational groupings, comprising past and present pupils of Vickerstown Primary School on Walney Island – groups consisting of individuals aged between 10 and 86. Our aim as facilitators was to encourage, stimulate and provoke high-level thinking, reflection, speaking and listening in the groups, but to avoid (insofar as this is ever possible) displaying our own views and beliefs. That said, we *did* aim to create environments in which individual members of the groups influenced each other's thinking. Individuals who found and who could articulate good reasons for changing their minds were valued for the honesty of their determination to find the best resolution of the dilemma, not despised for capitulating to someone else's 'bigger brain',  dominating personality or strongly expressed opinion. In this way, we tried to harness the best, most transformative and fluid characteristics of group learning processes, and to discourage the emergence of unhelpful 'right-wrong', 'clever-stupid', 'popular-isolated' dualities.

We set identical tasks for both adults and children, but differentiated the chosen dilemma and the instructions to suit the needs of the groups involved. Typically, the enquiries took the form described below:

## What are wise skills?

- Read the dilemma provided.
- Consider how the main character in this dilemma should respond.
- Now reflect upon and list the skills and abilities that you drew upon to make your decision as wise as possible.

When we asked teachers, other adults and children/young people to do tasks like this, they offered a range of skills and abilities that we termed 'wise skills and dispositions'. It emerged that the same skills and abilities were being elicited independently across all groups, irrespective of the dilemma used as the stimulus or the age of the group participants. However, the specific terminology used was influenced by age, experience and educational levels. The wise skills and dispositions can be summarised in the form of four broad themes, which can be seen to relate to three broad domains of 'being a whole person' and the evaluative domain of wise judgement – which calls upon the integration of the first three domains:

---

### Wise skills and dispositions

**Thinking and reflection** – eg logical and analytical thinking, planning and organisation, creative thinking, using past experience and knowledge, curiosity and wonder, enquiry

**Working, playing and living together** – eg sociability, belonging to a community, teamwork, communication, empathy

**Feeling good about ourselves** – eg independence, self-esteem, emotional resilience and wellbeing, persistence, motivation

**Making wise choices** – eg keeping a balance, taking reasonable risks, decision-making, being honest, good judgement

---

Whilst the first three themes were half-anticipated by ourselves, corresponding as they do to the cognitive, social and emotional ontological domains, the fourth theme emerged more slowly from our interrogation of the emergent data. As the notion of 'making wise choices' emerged, we struggled to find a way first of integrating, then of using it in an educationally congruent way. The Yale psychologist Robert Sternberg provided a model  when he outlined his 'balance theory of wisdom' (Sternberg, 2000). This theory incorporates practical, inter-personal, intra-personal and extra-personal interests within the same model and provides a starting point to consider the core skills and abilities required to be an effective and humane person at school and in society.

Sternberg has noted that:

> *The ultimate test of whether a judgement is wise is in how the judgement is made, rather than in what the judgement is. Two individuals can come to different conclusions, but both be wise if they fulfil the criteria specified by the balance theory.*

(STERNBERG, 2000)

Another eminent psychologist, the Harvard academic Howard Gardner, has made a related observation, again valuing the process and breadth of the enquiry rather than the end product:

> *The defining characteristic of wisdom is the breadth of considerations taken into account when rendering a judgment or recommending a course of action.*

(GARDNER, 1999)

For Sternberg, Gardner and others working in or around the fringes of the modern movement of 'positive psychology,' the task of life is to harness our gifts, talents, skills, dispositions and virtues in the major realms of living (eg learning, work, love, parenting) and to seek to live a 'meaningful life', which Martin Seligman describes as the 'use of your strengths and virtues in the service of something much larger than you are' (Seligman, 2003). However, both Sternberg and Gardner have questioned the extent to which we teach, value and model truly wise behaviour in our schools and in our society (cf Sternberg, 2002; Gardner et al, 2001). The challenge, for us, was to consider how to promote the emergence of wise skills, abilities and dispositions in our schools, not in instrumental, linear, *you-need-to-know-this* terms, but in a way that might engage the learners in the creation of their own knowledge. Mirroring differing approaches to the development of thinking skills per se (cf McGuinness, 1999) there are two mechanisms for transmission:

**i.** explicit teaching within a discrete lesson

**ii.** an across-the-curriculum 'infusion' model.

The first mechanism characterises approaches to thinking skills developed in the UK, Israel and America by, amongst others, de Bono (eg CoRT, Six Thinking Hats, cf de Bono 1978, 1987, 2000), Blagg (Somerset Thinking Skills, cf Blagg et al, 1988), Feuerstein (Instrumental Enrichment, cf Feuerstein, 1980), and Lipman (Philosophy for Children, cf Lipman, 1993, 2003), whereas the infusion model is more characteristic of the work of Swartz and Parks (cf Swartz and Parks, 1994), David Perkins (cf Perkins, 1992, 1995; Tishman et al, 1995), Art Costa (cf Costa, 2001), Steve Higgins (cf Higgins and Baumfield, 1998), Socratic questioning (cf Fisher, 2003), and the work of Carol McGuinness herself (the ACTS Project, cf McGuinness et al, 1996).

While we believed that an infusion approach held perhaps the greatest potential for the creation of wise learning communities, we also held that the only way to be truly effective is to place these skills and dispositions at the heart of what we do, in all areas of school life, irrespective of the methodology chosen. One possible way of looking at this is as a triad of approaches as shown below in figure 1.

**Figure. 1: Triad of intervention**

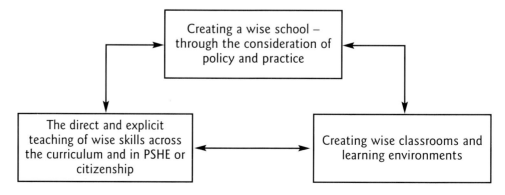

None of the three elements of the triad should confuse wise skills and wise behaviour with other abstract concepts, such as intelligence or personality. This is deliberate, and based on such evidence as provided in decades of research in the field by Baltes and Kunzmann:

> *Wisdom ... is not a primarily cognitive phenomenon. Rather, our analyses suggest that wisdom involves cognitive, emotional and motivational characteristics, and is a variant neither of intelligence nor of personality dimensions that can be assessed with psychometric tests.*
>
> (BALTES AND KUNZMANN, 2003.)

Baltes and Kunzmann's work with adults seemed to mirror our early and much less comprehensive developmental work with children, young people *and* adults – behaving wisely is, we held, about integrating multiple domains of knowledge and experience, and should be within the province of all.

## Creating wise learning opportunities

If wise skills are not only caught by osmosis but underpinned by a body of skills, values and understandings, these should be valued in the curriculum. They might be seen as the skills and abilities that underpin high-quality learning in citizenship and PSHE, but they might also be taught within tutorial sessions or planned across the curriculum[1]. However, we made no attempt to compile an exhaustive list of these skills and dispositions or define them. We trusted that in providing a rich and engaging task, and the space to wrestle this task into the open, the requisite skills, dispositions and values would be called upon and developed. Bruner identified the difficulty in this way:

> [1] The SEAL and SEBS materials currently being introduced into schools in England reflect much of the thinking underpinning the BarroWise Project and the development of the Webs of Meaning approach. This is in large part through the influence of Deborah Michel, who went on to become a lead author of the SEAL materials for the DCSF.

> *To isolate the major difficulty, then, I would say that while a body of knowledge is given life and direction by the conjectures and dilemmas that brought it into being and sustained its growth, pupils who are being taught often do not have a corresponding sense of conjecture and dilemma. The task of the curriculum maker and teacher is to provide exercises and occasions for its nurturing. If one only thinks of materials and content, one can all too easily overlook the problem. I believe it is precisely because instruction takes the form of telling-out-of-the-context-of-action that the difficulty emerges. The answer is the design of exercises in conjecture, in ways of inquiry, in problem-finding. It is something that the good teacher does naturally at least some of the time. With help from the curriculum-maker's exercises and conjectures, it is something that ordinary teachers will do much more of the time.*
>
> (BRUNER, 1966)

How did we seek to ensure that we covered the 'wise' decision-making skills and abilities? In some Barrow primary schools staff chose to identify a 'wise' focus for each half-term and then for each week a key learning outcome was identified, which was taught and promoted within PSHE and across the curriculum. Others looked to ways of incorporating wise skills and dispositions in their pedagogies. It was found that some pedagogical approaches lent themselves more effectively to promoting the wise skills than others. Examples of approaches that lent themselves well to 'wise work' included:

- experiential group work
- circle time
- philosophy for children
- drama techniques
- Webs of Meaning through dilemma-based learning.

Webs of Meaning became a development of our initial work in addressing the BarroWise question. We developed the Webs of Meaning approach, building on our exploratory work with dilemmas, because it struck us as being a fruitful area for enquiry-based exploration for many reasons, including the following:

- it involves 'real' problems, which we all face in some form in our day-to-day lives (the Nietzschean notion that the most instructive experiences are those of everyday life)

- it supports the development of 'learning dispositions' – attitudes to learning that are essential prerequisites for high-level performances – dispositions such as emotional resilience, coping with complexity and ambiguity, and persistence
- it is open-ended: there is rarely one, absolute, objectively best response that is immediately apparent to all learners. The best response is that which emerges successfully from the crucible of the group enquiry – cf Vygotsky's *Mind in Society* (1978) – having been tested, adapted and transformed during this process
- it values the creation of divergent, generative solutions, while also requiring these solutions to be tested against real-life constraints and implications
- because of its open-ended nature, it invites rich, textured and collaborative discussion, differentiated according to the experiences and abilities of the individuals participating in these enquiries
- because of its open-ended nature, there is a greater emphasis on learning and collaboration, and less of an emphasis on performance and competition
- it invites the application and development of reasoning and other thinking skills, and a wide range of social and emotional skills – ie most, if not all, of the *wise skills and dispositions* identified on p159
- it requires the progression of discussion to the point of a reasoned and reasonable conclusion, through the weighing of evidence, implications, and possible consequences
- it includes an emphasis on pro-social, community-centred resolutions, not just those offering the quickest fix or biggest gains for the few. In this way, resolutions are valued that are seen as wise, not just clever
- it values the involvement and inclusion of all members of the group, including those with literacy, attentional and behavioural difficulties. In our experience, children with special educational needs seem to derive particular benefit and enjoyment from Webs of Meaning activities
- it is intrinsically motivating to children and adults.

Finally, whilst the Webs of Meaning approach does not set out explicitly to 'teach wisdom,' it does, we believe, come very close to mirroring Baltes and Kunzmann's definition of wisdom as 'expert knowledge and judgement about important, difficult and uncertain questions associated with the meaning and conduct of life' (Baltes and Kunzmann, 2003). To test for wisdom, Baltes and Kunzmann presented people with difficult hypothetical situations and used a standardised procedure to collect think-aloud responses. These tasks differed from tasks associated with intelligence-testing in that they were deliberately poorly defined and characterised by multiple solutions. As Baltes and Kunzmann themselves note, 'High-quality responses to these situations therefore require exceptional intellectual and social-emotional abilities' (ibid). And these abilities, we believe, can be developed in children through regular, supported exposure to Webs of Meaning experiences – the approach is less about testing than learning.

The Webs of Meaning represent, as far as possible, an antidote to the 'body of good knowledge' approach to education. To this end, participants are encouraged to acquire the skills that will allow them to interrogate knowledge, assess its 'goodness' and arrive at reasonable judgements based on the consideration of multiple criteria. This involves not just coping with but also valuing uncertainty, as Dewey advocated: 'Dewey was unusual in that he accepted uncertainty and the open and dynamic nature of life. (He) was one of the first to struggle with the messiness and complexity of human learning and development' (Abbott and Ryan, 2000). Students are encouraged to work towards, in David Perkins' (1995) term, 'a pedagogy of understanding'. Perkins has identified the features of topics that lend themselves better than others to a 'pedagogy of understanding'. Such topics are, he believes, 'generative': they invite understanding performances of various kinds, and make teaching for understanding easy. A good generative topic, Perkins (ibid) believes, embodies three standards:

- **Centrality** – the topic should be central to a subject matter or curriculum.
- **Accessibility** – the topic should allow and invite teachers' and students' understanding (not just knowing) performances.
- **Richness** – the topic should encourage a rich play of varied extrapolation and connection-making.

Our dilemmas, we believe, meet Perkins' standards for a good generative topic: they are beyond the baseline of content knowledge, and they are central to all curriculum areas – dilemmas abound, for instance, in history, drama, English literature, science and mathematics, and if we choose not to confront or even to recognize them, our mastery of the subject matter is diminished greatly. As recalled by Bruner:

> I took a group of 14-year-olds to see Peter Ustinov's Billy Budd on film. The intensity of the discussion of moral philosophy on the way home convinced me that we have overlooked one of our most powerful allies in keeping our engagement in history, in the range of human life, in philosophy. Drama, the novel, history, are all built on the paradox of human choice, on the resolution of alternatives. They are in the best sense studies in the causes and consequences of choice. It is in their gripping quality, their nearness to life, that we can best make personal the dilemmas of the culture, its aspirations, its conflicts, its terrors. In some considerable measure we have intellectualised and made bland and good-natured the teaching of the particulars of history, of society, of myth.
>
> (BRUNER, 1966)

Of course, not all dilemmas take the forms embodied in the PSHE or citizenship curricula, but whilst their outworkings may be subject specific, the principles of their resolution are pretty much universal. Subject specific dilemmas in the secondary humanities are the focus of this book.

Secondly, dilemmas not only allow and invite understanding performances, they demand it. Merely to list a series of possible solutions or to state a preferred solution is inadequate. Students must, in order to resolve a dilemma, make use of the following examples of understanding performances:

- **explain** a possible solution in their own words
- **provide examples** of possible implications or consequences
- **apply** their ideas in new or evolving situations
- **justify** their preferences
- **compare and contrast** one solution with another
- **contextualise** a solution within a wider framework (eg community needs)
- **generalise** from one solution to a wider social or moral truth.

Such a list could be extended. Work at this level of thinking requires an individual to make explicit the nature of their thinking.

Finally, dilemmas seem to us to be almost absurdly rich in their possibilities for extrapolation and connection-making. Children, given the opportunity, seem to have few difficulties exercising their human capacity for discovering meaning, exposing apparent contradictions by drawing parallels between and across fields, sometimes with devastating and unnerving accuracy. For example, during one dilemma-based enquiry with nine-year-olds, the issue of under-age smoking was addressed. The group, having moved towards a collaborative and shared understanding of the long-term consequences of this behaviour, was pulled up short by the observation of one child, who'd been relatively quiet until that point. She said simply, 'We've decided that smoking is bad for us in our future, yeah? But I'm puzzled. Why then do so many adults say to me I should live life for today?'

To the insights of philosophers like Burgh, novelists like Atwood and educationists like Perkins and Baumfield et al (2005), might be added another, related justification for encouraging students to engage critically in their education – a critical, dialogically based education supports the development of life-skills that are useful in their own right. Tenzin Gyatso, the Dalai Lama, captures this well:

> *I do believe that dialogue can and should be taught in class. Presenting students with a controversial issue and having them debate it is a wonderful way to introduce them to the concept of resolving conflict non-violently. Indeed, one would hope that if schools were to make this a priority, it could have a beneficial effect on family life itself. On seeing his or her parents wrangling, a child that had understood the value of dialogue would instinctively say, 'Oh no. That's not the way. You have to talk, to discuss things properly.'*

(GYATSO, 1999)

Our intention in creating the Webs of Meaning approach, and the resource you are reading, is to assist us in this task. May we all talk, and discuss things properly.

## The contributions that dilemma-based learning can make to the new secondary curriculum

In September 2007, the new secondary curriculum was unveiled so that schools can prepare for its implementation in 2008. The aims of the curriculum are to develop: successful learners, confident individuals, responsible citizens. It encourages schools to consider attitudes, attributes and skills as well as knowledge and understanding and provides a clear steer for all subjects to promote personal development and personal learning and thinking skills (PLTS). This new emphasis will be a challenge to subject teachers who have up to now had a purely subject-based approach. Dilemma-based learning provides a powerful vehicle to support subject teachers as they adapt to the new curriculum and its expectation that they will support the development of the curriculum aims, personal development and personal learning and thinking skills.

*Chris Kington Publishing*

# Bibliography

Abbott, J and Ryan, T (2000) *The Unfinished Revolution: Learning, human behaviour, community and political paradox,* Stafford: Network Educational Press

Baltes, PB and Kunzmann, U (2003) 'Wisdom', *The Psychologist,* 16, 3, pp131-132

Blagg, N, Ballinger, M and Gardner, R (1988) *Somerset Thinking Skills Course: Handbook,* Oxford: Basil Blackwell

Bruner, JS (1966) *Toward a Theory of Instruction,* Cambridge, MA: Harvard University Press

Burgh, G (2003) 'P4C in Middle East' – email to an international Philosophy for Children web-based discussion group, submitted on 3 February 2003

Costa, A (2001) *Developing Minds – A resource book for teaching thinking,* Alexandria Virginia: Association for Supervision and Curriculum Development

Dadds, M (2001) 'Politics of pedagogy: the state and children', *Teachers and Teaching: Theory and Practice,* 7, 1, pp49-53

de Bono, E (1978) *Teaching Thinking,* Harmondsworth: Penguin Books

de Bono, E (1987) *CoRT Thinking Program – workcards and teacher's notes,* Chicago: Science Research Associates

de Bono, E (2000) *Six Thinking Hats,* London: Penguin Books

Feuerstein, R, Rand, Y, Hoffman, MB and Miller, R (1980) *Instrumental Enrichment: An intervention for cognitive modifiability,* Baltimore, MD: University Park Press

Fisher, R (2003) *Teaching Thinking* (2nd edition), London: Continuum

Gardner, H (1999) *Intelligence Reframed – Multiple intelligences for the 21st century,* New York: Basic Books

Gardner, H, Csikszentmihalyi, M and Damon, W (2001) *Good Work – When Excellence and Ethics Meet,* New York: Basic Books

Gould, SJ (1984) *The Mismeasure of Man,* London: Penguin Books

Gyatso, T (1999) *Ancient Wisdom, Modern World – Ethics for a New Millennium,* London: Abacus

Higgins, S, Hall, E, Baumfield, V, Moseley, D (2005) 'A meta-analysis of the impact of the implementation of thinking skills approaches on pupils', in *Research Evidence in Education Library,* London: EPPI Centre, Social Science Research Unit, Institute of Education, University of London

Higgins, S and Baumfield, V (1998) 'A defence of teaching general thinking skills', *Journal of Philosophy of Education,* 32, 3, pp391-398

Holzman, L (1997) *Schools for Growth - Radical alternatives to current educational models,* New Jersey: Lawrence Erlbaum Associates

Lipman, M (ed) (1993) *Thinking Children and Education,* Iowa: Kendall-Hunt

Lipman, M (2003) *Thinking in Education,* Cambridge: Cambridge University Press

McGuinness, C (1999) 'From Thinking Skills to Thinking Classrooms: A review and evaluation of approaches for developing students' thinking' *(DfEE Research Report RR115)* Nottingham: DfEE Publications

McGuinness, C, Curry, C, Greer, B, Daly, P and Salters, M (1996) Final report on ACTS Project: Phase 1, submitted to Northern Ireland Council for Curriculum, Examination and Assessment

Perkins, D (1992) *Smart Schools: Better thinking and learning for every child,* New York: The Free Press

Perkins, D (1995) *Outsmarting IQ: The Emerging Science of Learnable Intelligence,* New York: The Free Press

Potts, R (2003) 'Light in the wilderness – a profile of Margaret Atwood', *The Guardian Review,* 26 April 2003, pp20-23

Seligman, ME (2003) 'Positive Psychology – fundamental assumptions', *The Psychologist,* 16, 3, pp126-127

Sternberg, RJ (2000) 'Wisdom as a form of giftedness', *Gifted Child Quarterly,* 44, 4, pp252-260

Sternberg, RJ (ed) (2002) *Why Smart People Can Be So Stupid,* New Haven: Yale University Press

Swartz, R and Parks, S (1994) *Infusing the Teaching of Critical and Creative Thinking Into Content Instruction: A lesson design handbook for elementary grades,* California: Critical Thinking Press & Software

Tishman, S, Perkins, D and Jay, E (1995) *The Thinking Classroom: Learning and teaching in a culture of thinking,* Boston: Allyn & Bacon

Vygotsky, LS (1978) *Mind in Society,* Cambridge MA: Harvard University Press

# Webs of Meaning
# photocopiable resource

# The Web of Meaning

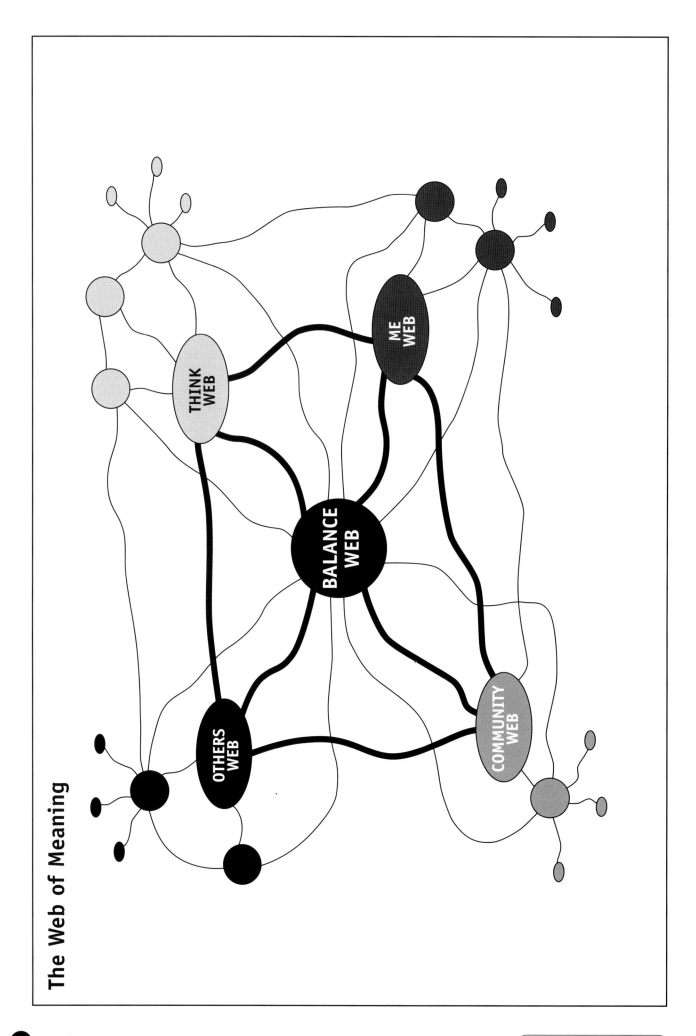

Chris Kington Publishing

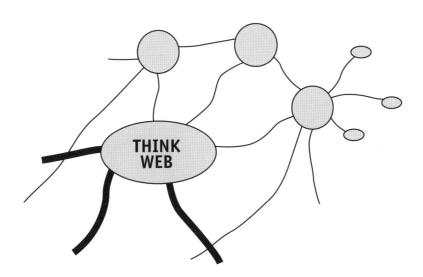

# The Think Web

This Web has three main elements. The first step is an opportunity for reflection and analysis. Ask yourself:

- Is this a dilemma? What makes this a dilemma?
- What are the key issues that might influence a solution?
- How does this dilemma resemble something I've encountered before?

The second step is to generate as many possible solutions to the dilemma as possible – be creative. Ask yourself:

- How many solutions can we find?
- Can any solutions be linked or connected in some way, to form yet another solution?
- Can we think of any more unusual ideas?

The third step is to select the three most practical solutions. Ask yourself:

- Are any of the solutions clearly unrealistic? Are you sure?
  How do you know this?
- What exactly is involved in each solution?
- What would happen if this were to be done?
- How would we know if it were successful?
- What would happen if we tried and failed?
- How likely is it to be successful?
- Which three shall we choose?
- What are the costs – time, money, etc?

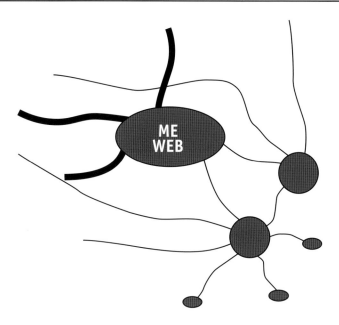

# The Me Web

The first step is to establish each group member's personal feelings. Ask:

- How does everyone feel about the choice of solutions?
- Are there any objections to the choices made by the group? On what grounds?
- Do you have anything you wish to say from your own point of view or experience?

The second step is to explore each of the chosen options from the perspective of the central character in the dilemma. Ask:

- How would he or she feel?
- What would it mean for him or her?
- What would happen to him or her as a result of the actions?

One member of your group could take the role of the central character for the discussion.

Chris Kington Publishing

# The Others Web

The first step is to identify which other characters might be affected by the dilemma or the solutions identified. Ask:

- Who else is mentioned in the dilemma?
- Is there anyone else who might be affected, but who isn't specifically mentioned?

The second step is to explore the dilemma from the perspective of each of the minor characters identified, examining each of the three 'solutions' in turn. Ask:

- What would happen to the character?
- How would the character feel?
- How would the character feel if he or she found out what had happened?
- What would each character like to happen?
- What does each character know about the dilemma and the suggested solution?

Each member of your group could take on the role of one of the characters for this discussion.

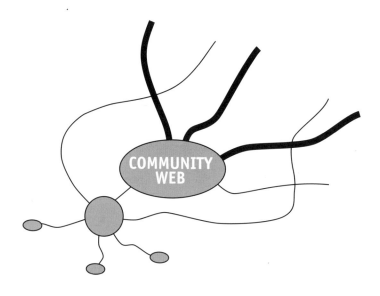

# The Community Web

This Web gives your group an opportunity to explore what the various options might mean for the community as a whole. Ask:

- What would happen if everyone chose to do this?
- What would people think about the family/class/school?
- How would the situation look to other people?
- What would happen in the long term to the family/class/school?
- What might other people in the community learn from what had happened?

Chris Kington Publishing

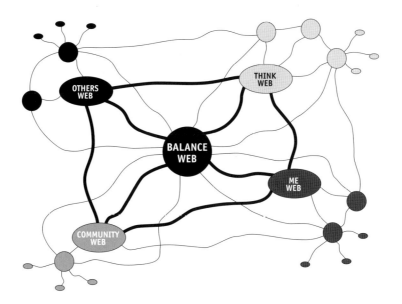

# The Balance Web

This Web allows time for reflection to make a balanced choice. The first step is for each member of your group to reflect individually on their intuitive choices.

The second step is for each member to specify his or her preferred option – listen carefully without interrupting when other members are speaking.

If there is no consensus, everyone should restate their preferred option – providing reasons. This time, other members of the group can ask questions to explore the implications of the solution. Ask:

- What would happen if this solution worked?
- What might go wrong and why?
- What might happen if the solution went wrong?
- How likely is it that the solution might go wrong?
- How likely is it that the solution would work?
- Is the solution practical?

If there is a consensus, your group could quickly review the implications of the chosen solution by working through the previous Webs.

Chris Kington Publishing